CORPORATE
KARMA

CORPORATE KARMA

How Business Can
Move Forward
by Giving Back

PEGGIE PELOSI

Foreword by Lance H. K. Secretan

ORENDA

Cataloguing in Publication Data
available from Archives Canada

Pelosi, Peggie
Corporate Karma: How business can move
forward by giving back

ISBN-13 978-0-9782327-0-2

Cover design: Angel Guerra/Archetype
Author photograph: Yanka Van der Kolk
Text design: Tannice Goddard, Soul Oasis Networking

Printed on 100% recycled paper

100% of net proceeds of Corporate Karma will be contributed
to a number of foundations and humanitarian organizations
that support local and international leadership and
economic development programs for women and children.

Printed and bound in Canada

Published by
ORENDA PUBLISHING
Toronto, Canada

For my dad,
John A. McArthur,
for giving me roots and wings

Contents

Foreword

We live in a society that has revered corporate Darwinism. But the tide is changing. A stirring of people's hearts has begun. Corporate success achieved solely through ruthless and aggressive acquisition of new customers and the domination of markets is disappointing and even repelling the very customers and employees that organizations struggle to come by. A new yearning is stirring within us to replace corporate self-interest with service that honors others and the environment. As Shirley Chisholm says, "Service is the rent that you pay for room on this earth."

Those who dream of a brighter, more inspiring and compassionate future for humanity realize that organizations — especially business entities — are the most powerful institutions on the planet because they possess an unmatched opportunity to change the world. In fact if we really wanted to change the world sooner rather than later, the most expedient method would be to change the way Wal-Mart, Exxon, GE and General Motors do business, because they employ millions, touch billions and reach everywhere. By adapting just these four powerful institutions we would immediately adapt the world.

Organizations that think this way (and many already do) become serving organizations that inspire and attract people, no longer needing to aggressively pursue them.

The flow is reversed — the laws of the warrior are replaced with the laws of attraction. Costs plummet — marketing, recruiting and the costs of replenishing defecting employees and customers are replaced by a steady, low-cost flow of customers seeking to be served and people moved to join these inspiring teams.

I have seen organizations slash their operating costs by hundreds of millions of dollars through this simple change in philosophy.

In 1997 I was privileged to chair the advisory board of the Special Olympics World Winter Games. Special Olympics, named "the most credible charity in North America" by the *Journal of Philanthropy*, is the largest international program dedicated to children and adults with intellectual disabilities. Conceived by Eunice Kennedy Shriver and Sargent Shriver 35 years ago and supported by the Joseph Kennedy Foundation, the program today sees over 2.5 million intellectually handicapped athletes training and participating in over 30 Olympic-type sporting events in 200 programs in 150 countries.

The mission of the Special Olympics is to provide year-round sports training and athletic events to these Special Olympians, and they are called "special" for a good reason. The looks on the faces of the athletes tell it all. When they receive their medals, when they assist a fallen contestant, when they celebrate the triumph of their will over their mental challenges and when they hug their families, coaches and friends, the tides of joy flooding their hearts, though evident, can only be imagined by others. The hearts of volunteers and sponsors burst no less with pride and love for them, too.

For Special Olympians, there are no contract lawyers, no multi-million-dollar endorsement deals, no tantrums and no egos — just big hearts and beautiful souls.

I learned a lesson about the power of corporate philanthropy from Jean-Pierre van Rooy, then president of Otis Elevator. A division of United Technologies, the company is the world's largest elevator manufacturer, employing 60,000 people who guide two million elevators and 100,000 escalators in 200 countries. United Technologies had supported Special Olympics for many years, and when "J.P." was transferred from Europe to become the president of Otis, he was asked to attend a Sunday track-and-field event sponsored by the company. He described it as one of the best days of his life, and he made a spontaneous personal commitment to participate every year in the future.

In 1994 United Technologies made a cash commitment to Special Olympics of $1 million, of which Otis pledged $250,000. J.P. was not looking for an opportunity to support a charity — he was looking for a partner that would involve all of Otis's international employees as volunteers in a worthy and noble venture. One year later this ambitious initiative resulted in Team Otis embracing 4,000 Otis employees from operations in 38 countries who were deeply committed to supporting the games — coaching, fundraising, assisting athletes, finding sponsors and managing events.

In addition to the corporate pledge, another $350,000 was raised through employee contributions, and many national operations of Otis defrayed the travel costs of their country's athletes, enabling Malaysia, for example, to participate in the games for the first time. Over 100 Otis employees from 27 countries, many of them traveling with their nation's Special Olympic team, joined with 600 United States–based volunteers at New Haven where they worked around the clock, creating unparalleled camaraderie among themselves and celebrating the gifts of intellectually challenged athletes.

As J.P. said to me later, Otis had participated in many team-building and leadership programs, but none came close to matching the results of the partnership between Otis and Special Olympics. It cut across all boundaries of race, country, creed, function and division; hierarchies disappeared and previously undiscovered leaders emerged. People who had never met each other, and had no reason to, suddenly became partners in a noble cause, united as brothers and sisters in an inspiring organization.

How does one measure the impact of such a venture on the bottom line? Perhaps one should not try. The lessons learned through cooperation, sharing a vision, helping others to realize their dreams, forming new friendships and striving without competition have all been immense for Otis. The strengthening of internal morale and the lessons of leadership and activity management have yielded growing and lasting benefits for everyone — on and off the job. Team Otis was so exhilarated by their experience that they made a long-term commitment to their partnership with Special Olympics, creating a legacy that will affect the lives of millions of people for many years. From this they are profiting today, and will continue to do so, in their financial statements and their souls. That is the bottom line.

This is what Peggie Pelosi has so succinctly called corporate karma — what goes around, comes around. For too long we have sown — and therefore reaped — fear in the workplace and adversarial competition in the marketplace, mistakenly believing that this leads to success. Peggie brings her unique experience of building the reputation, culture and revenues of a major corporation with leadership skills that include corporate philanthropy. Her message is a unique one, complete with practical advice — showing us how to succeed in a way that inspires.

Dr. Lance H. K. Secretan
BESTSELLING AUTHOR ON INSPIRING LEADERSHIP

Acknowledgments

I have often thought about writing a book. Different subjects have come to mind at different times along my journey. It wasn't until my work with Orenda, however, that I knew I had something truly of value to say. All through this there have been many constants along my path. I am so grateful to:

My mother, Ruth McArthur, for, among many things, insisting that I eat all my peas. My five beautiful sons, Adrian, Luke, Jordan, Michael and Jonathan, for their constant support and inspiration. Thomas Gardiner, for caring and understanding. Lucy and Stella, for unconditional love and protection. Jake McArthur, for coaching and confidence. My guardian angel Sol Bienstock, for all he taught me along the way. My friends Tricia and Lance Secretan, for their encouragement, mentoring and love over the years.

I would also like to express my deep gratitude to all those who have helped bring *Corporate Karma* to life:

Dr. Myron Wentz, chairman and CEO of USANA Health Sciences, and Dave Phillips, president of Children's Hunger Fund™, for giving me the opportunity to discover this purpose and passion.

And to our clients, collaborators and contributors:

Pat Bjerrisgaard, senior director, Community, Business Objects; Kathryn Babcock, senior director, Communications and Corporate Development, Canadian Women's Foundation; John Reid, executive director, and Sarah Rodriguez, vice president, Corporate and Chapter Relations, Childhelp; Mitchell Wade, CEO, and Emily Franson, director, Expeditions and Community Outreach, Choice Humanitarian; Elaine Dembe; Elaine Weidman, director of Corporate Responsibility, Ericsson, and Dag Nielsen, Ericsson Response; Peggy Willett, Getty Images; Linda Ginou; Noni Verbiscar-Brown, resource specialist, Catherine Kirby, COO, and Peter Verbiscar-Brown, executive director, Global Partners for Development; Karen Davis, vice president, Community Relations, Hasbro; Brad Shaw, SVP, Corporate Communications and External Affairs, The Home Depot; Peter McArthur; Peter Broder, Imagine Canada; John Anderson, Jim and Kathy Coover, co-founders, Jim Pierce, COO, Isagenix International; Dr. John Izzo, The Izzo Group; Robert Kent, Robert Kent Photography, and the team at the Compassionate Eye Foundation; Susan Knobler, Give the Gift of Sight, LensCrafters/Luxottica; Craig Cinchy, manager, M·A·C Aids Fund; Mark Sarner, president, Manifest Communications; Jeffrey Flug, CEO, Millennium Promise Alliance; Janice Gerol, vice president and general manager,

The Pampered Chef; Don Green, co-founder, and Robert Sarner, director, Communications and Public Affairs, Roots; Deeva Green, for her beautiful inspiration, and Sophie "loves" Green for inspiring Michael; Ryan Hreljac and Beth Morey, Ryan's Well Foundation; Renee Safrata and Jim Sellner; Mitchell Gallinger, president, and Lori Lord, COO, Spectrum Health Care; Jeffrey Swartz, president and CEO, and Kate King, Corporate Communications, Timberland; Cynthia Kersey, Unstoppable Enterprises Inc.; Dave Mowat, CEO, and Paula Martin, vice president, Public Affairs and Corporate Communications, Vancity; Dr. Denis Waitley, The Waitley Institute; Tonika Morgan, Women Moving Forward; Ari Weinzwerg, Zingerman's Community of Businesses.

Thanks also to the *Corporate Karma*/Orenda team:

Phil Thompson, legal eagle, Thompson, Dymond; Hilary Roberts, researcher and great daughter-in-law; Janice Waugh, writer, WORDS; Tannice Goddard, text designer, Soul Oasis Networking; Angel Guerra, artist and designer, Archetype Design Communications; Don Bastian, tireless writer and editor, Bastian Publishing Services Ltd.; Jodi Lastman, brilliant researcher, writer and collaborator; Arnold Gosewich, conductor, director, and publishing consultant extraordinaire.

And finally, a big thank you to all the inspiring people at the companies and causes who are connecting to make our world a better place.

Never doubt that a small group of thoughtful citizens can change the world. Indeed, it is the only thing that ever has.

— MARGARET MEAD

Introduction

More and more leaders are beginning to understand a very basic but very powerful formula: companies that give back become companies that move forward.

I'm not talking about giving back in the old way, in which a board or committee, remote from the needs of their community, dispenses checks with little or no input from other members of the company — and little or no connection to the people benefiting from their benevolence. I'm talking about a new form of corporate philanthropy in which an entire company becomes engaged in finding, choosing and serving a cause. A new form of philanthropy in which the inspirational energy that is released by reaching out to those in need spills back into the company itself.

This way of giving results at the micro level in more caring, engaged employees. And it results at the macro level in senior executives and boards who temper their objectives and strategies with a sense of purpose much greater than quarterly earnings and market share.

This new philanthropy and its beneficial effects in the world and in companies are what this book is about.

It is first of all a why-to book. In the first part I share my own story of coming to see how companies can give back and move forward. This part of the book goes on to help you find your company's soul and challenges you to make it manifest in the world through giving, with intention, to a worthy cause. It shows that companies can achieve a shift in collective consciousness, why this is important and the effect it has on all concerned.

But this book is also a how-to book. The second part of the book shows you as leaders how to meaningfully integrate a corporate philanthropy program into your workplace. It gives you a step-by-step guide for creating a strategic philanthropy program and embedding it into your company.

The third, and final, part of the book is a colorful tapestry of attitudes and actions regarding giving together as companies. You'll hear the voices of the young employees of the future who are entering companies with a philanthropic philosophy already in place, of former business executives who are exiting the corporate world for more meaningful work and of non-profit leaders. All of these people and groups offer different perspectives on the best and most meaningful ways to connect company and cause. In the final chapter you'll read, more specifically, a collection of inspiring real-life stories from great companies who are doing well while doing good.

My prediction is that you are going to become more and more inspired as you turn the pages of this book and get an inside look at the realities, and possibilities, of making a difference while making a living.

PART 1

Why Give Together?

On a Clear Day
I Can See Africa
The Orenda Story

Don't say that you want to give, but go ahead and give!
You'll never catch up with a mere hope.
— GOETHE

In 2000, after a long and successful career in sales, I accepted a position as vice president of Network Development (sales) for USANA Health Sciences. In joining this public company, a manufacturer and distributor of nutritional supplements based in Utah, I was also accepting my first "job job": the kind that required me to go to an office and work closely with colleagues on a shared vision. When I accepted the assignment I was accepting a significant challenge. The company had experienced flat sales during the previous few years, despite aggressive international expansion. It was looking to me to re-energize the sales force and turn things around.

I was to stay with USANA until 2004. It was immediately evident to me when I started that something was fundamentally wrong with the company's culture. Rather than embracing its mission to "develop and provide the highest quality, science-based health products," it was engaged in office politics, the effect of which inevitably trickled down to the entire sales force. I knew that addressing the company's culture would do more than anything else to breathe new life into the organization. I wondered what would happen if every person who worked for and with USANA was completely energized by the company's mission and its founder's ultimate dream of "a world free from pain and suffering ... a world free from disease." What if that's what drove people? What if that's what they woke up to do every day?

During my short time at USANA I created and integrated into its corporate culture a philanthropy program that changed the way people felt about the company they worked for. USANA partnered with Children's Hunger Fund™ to get desperately needed nutritional supplements to children in the developing world. CHF has an on-the-ground presence in many developing countries. They could see the remarkable changes that our supplements were making in the lives of children ravaged by disease and hunger, and they shared their stories with those of us who were energized with a new sense of purpose.

Through this partnership with CHF, USANA reached out to all of its employees, customers, board members and shareholders, who in turn donated both the company's nutritional supplements for children and their own financial resources. This had a profound impact on the company itself. I watched in awe as USANA's sales more than doubled, from $120 million to $270 million, and as its stock value rose over 3000%, from $1.70 to $70 a share.

Nothing had changed. The same people were in place, the same products were produced, the same marketing efforts were made. So what unlocked the potential of USANA? The only answer I could come up with was "good karma." The company had found its soul. People came to work for a higher purpose and were truly connected to the company's values.

At the same time donations to CHF during that period grew exponentially. In the first year of the program we contributed close to $120,000 in product and cash donations. By year three, as more and more constituents became engaged, the contributions grew to over $1 million.

What began as a philanthropy program became a way of life for USANA. What began as a partnership became an essential part of how it sees itself in the world. Today USANA's products continue to be distributed to children in need. I am proud to have been part of finding, and releasing, the company's soul. It has proved to be a win-win-win for children worldwide, for the numerous people who have had the life-changing experience of working for a company that touches their soul and for the shareholders of the company.

Karma and Giving

Karma is a sacred word in Sanskrit. It is used colloquially as the belief that "what goes around comes around." Ultimately it is an understanding that the energy that we give out, in thought, word or deed, good or bad, will somehow return to us. If what we give out is intended to inspire or improve the quality of life for someone or something, our generosity will reward us somehow. This is not the primary motive behind the act of generosity. But it is a core belief in how the universe operates, and it creates a positive context for giving.

Giving is good. Is this something we know intrinsically, or is it something we learn? When do we become conscious of the act of giving?

Someday I'll ...

When I was a little girl my mother insisted that I stay at the dinner table until I had eaten all my peas.

"There are starving children in Africa," she would say.

"Why can't we send them my peas?" I would ask.

Starving children was not a concept that I, growing up in a nice middle-class neighborhood in Toronto, could grasp. The milkman delivered milk to our home twice every week. I remember the bread truck coming up the driveway and the excitement over the Danish pastries my mom would buy as a treat from time to time. We'd go to Amodeo's fruits and vegetables to pick up our produce. I'd look in amazement through the glass cases at Clayton's, the butcher shop, not really understanding that those pork chops came from a pig, and listening to my mother chatting with the butcher about how tender the roast had been last week.

Starving children? Who were they and where were they and why didn't the milkman, the bread truck, Mr. Amodeo and the butcher just go there and give them what they needed?

The notion of starving children, although incomprehensible to me as a young girl, somehow did begin to register in my mind as I grew up. But this vague concept got filed away with all the other new areas of awareness that weave their way through the developing consciousness of a growing child.

Then throughout my youth I saw the Save the Children and World Vision advertisements on TV. Now I had a vision of starving children. I was not able to comprehend the full reality of this kind of suffering, but horrific images coupled with a call for help did give me a growing sense that there were needs beyond my own doorstep, and this was the genesis of a sense that I should be doing *something* to help.

The milkman and the bread truck stopped coming. The grocery stores got bigger and more abundant. The houses, cars and paychecks grew in value. In my own life the commitments and debts increased. With the rush of school, work, marriage, children, and mortgage and bills to pay, the vision of starving children dimmed. But it never disappeared. I wanted to help, but the timing was never right.

I have come to believe that reaching out to those in need is fundamental to human nature. We're created to want to help when we see suffering. Some make it a mission and build it into their life plan. However, most others, like me at the time, say, with the best of intentions, someday I'll:

- Get around to charity, when I've taken care of "me"
- Volunteer some time, when I have more of it
- Contribute some money, when I have enough myself
- Help those starving children in Africa, when I've taken care of my own

A Defining Moment

The journey to someday took a giant step forward for me in June 2004, when, after 30 hours in transit, I stepped out of the plane and reached down to touch the soil of Africa. I was on a business trip that would change my life forever.

I went to Africa with a group of 20 people who were part of or associated in some way with USANA Health Sciences, including the CEO of the company, Dr. Myron Wentz, board member Dr. Denis Waitley and my husband and five grown sons. We were there to lend a helping hand at an orphanage in Ggaba, a small fishing village on the shores of Lake Victoria, just outside Kampala, the capital city of Uganda.

For two weeks we all rolled up our sleeves and helped build the orphanage. We worked side by side with the local villagers, digging the trench for the water system, laying the brick for the home, helping in any way we could — not by doing the work for them but by doing it with them. We weren't there to tell them how to do things better. We were there to link arms with them, to say we do care and we do want to help. For two weeks our lives were blessed with the kindness, love, generosity and hospitality of a village that by our standards had nothing.

Once you've been to Africa, it stays with you.

The most vivid memories for me are the smiles. Ear to ear. Bigger than life. Smiles on the faces of children who had either lost one or both parents to disease, or who had been abandoned due to extreme poverty. Children who had nothing but the clothes on their backs, or if they were fortunate a thatched roof over their heads, perhaps a classroom filled with knowledge and wisdom and a community filled with love. The love comes through their smiles. They are grateful and they take nothing for granted. Each morning they would greet us, singing for us to welcome the day before they went off to school.

Africa is life changing. Anyone who has been there knows that. It puts the world in a new perspective. I can close my eyes and see it, smell it, touch it, hear it, feel it. I've often wondered why it is that Africa has such a profound impact on everyone who travels there.

The great biologist E.O. Wilson argues in several books and articles that human beings are hardwired to feel a special resonance with the African savannah, the place where our species arose some 150,000 years ago.

My friend Noni Verbiscar-Brown is a resource specialist at the non-profit Global Partners for Development, a humanitarian organization that works in Africa and that recently won the Albert Schweitzer Award of Excellence. Here, from an interview with Orenda, is how Noni explains this special connection to Africa:

> When people ask about our work, and I start to describe it, there is usually the question, "Why Africa?" My most frequent response is, "Because Africa has more of *it*."
>
> If you look at any of the indicators of human misery, the scales that societies use to judge suffering that could be alleviated if we had the will, Africa, especially sub-Saharan Africa, has more of *it*, whatever *it* is. Pick just about any indicator: lack of access to clean water, infant mortality, maternal mortality, low overall life expectancy, illiteracy (42 million

children do not have access to primary school), malnutrition — both protein deficiency and inadequate calories — lack of access to health care, morbidity of disease burden, Malaria/TB/ HIV prevalence, civil unrest, child soldiers, and on and on. Africa starts the 21st century as the poorest, the most technologically backward, the most debt distressed and the most marginalized region in the world. So why Africa? Because it is where the work is!

That trip to Africa was a defining moment in my life. Something that began as an opportunity to develop a strategic philanthropy program for the company I was working for turned into the beginning of a profound personal journey. I had found a way to send my peas to Africa ... while helping a business find its soul.

And to finally figure out why I was on the planet.

While galvanizing hundreds of people at USANA Health Sciences to contribute to Children's Hunger Fund™, I realized that our efforts were not only making a difference in the lives of children in the developing world, they were also helping us as employees to find greater meaning in our own lives.

The defining moment for me was in Africa, where the need is so great. But there are stories of making an extraordinary difference right in our own backyards. Meeting these needs creates an opportunity for giving for all businesses, large and small, to harness this power.

What If ...

We've heard the extraordinary stories of companies like Avon, Timberland and LensCrafters and how they have integrated giving programs into the very core of their businesses, transforming or defining their corporate culture in the process.

What if *every* company championed a cause?

What if every business leader gave employees and stakeholders the opportunity to link arms, tap a collective corporate soul and spread the mission of the company beyond the balance sheet and out into a world of need?

What if the curriculums of business schools taught that strategic corporate philanthropy and social responsibility are as integral to a business plan as finance and marketing?

What might that look like?

- Would employees be inspired?
- Would loyalty and retention increase?
- Would business attract great talent?
- Would the intrinsic common thread of compassion and inspiration weave its way through the tapestry of the corporate culture?
- Would leaders be enlightened?
- Would business grow?
- Would the world be just a little or a whole lot better?

The Business Case

This idea of strategic corporate philanthropy has been evolving under the concept of corporate social responsibility (CSR) for some time and is now reaching critical mass, or if you prefer, the tipping point. Business today is feeling the pressure to develop good corporate citizenship both from those in the talent pool looking for great companies to work for and consumers wanting to support companies that are community minded.

This is an idea whose time has come. Over a decade ago Paul Hawken, co-founder of the garden retailer Smith and Hawken, wrote the bestselling book *The Ecology of Commerce*. In it he brilliantly points out that the quality of every living system on earth is in decline as a direct result of personal and corporate irresponsibility. Our air and water are polluted, our forests are being destroyed and our animals are facing extinction. At the same time, human health is deteriorating, in part due to the stress and strain of the modern employee.

He goes on to predict that the trend will turn: there will be a profound business transformation, one that will render new business unrecognizable. The companies of the future will be in the business of healing our world. Businesses that exist to rebuild our communities, repair our ecosystems, protect the environment, improve our health and provide inspirational work environments that create prosperity, will thrive.

In the book and film *An Inconvenient Truth* Al Gore relates Hawken's message to the Chinese expression for crisis, which consists of two characters side by side. The first is "danger" and the second is "opportunity."

Corporations have become one of the most profound and influential forces on the planet. They are consolidating globally and forming massive multinationals. The balance of power today lies in their hands. Of the world's 100 largest economic entities 51 are corporations, and only 49 are countries, when measured by annual corporate sales and annual gross domestic product (GDP).

Corporations have an extraordinary opportunity to influence the world. Whether for good or bad — it's up to us.

Hawken's message has not only been heard, it has also been embraced. A collective consciousness is now demanding accountability.

Governments, businesses and individuals are being asked to step up.

Look Who's Talking

- Celebrities like Bono and Bill Clinton are relentlessly demanding action from world governments to end poverty,

AIDS and global warming
- Activists like George Clooney, Richard Gere and Angelina Jolie are encouraging all of us to take action, and are influencing a new generation
- Bill Gates and Warren Buffet are sending a clear message to the mega wealthy that we have to bridge this divide between the abundance of the few and the extreme need of the many

The list goes on, with these and other good people drawing our attention to the opportunity we all have as individuals to make a difference.

Meanwhile, the great business leaders are recognizing that success will no longer be measured by profit and share value alone, but by our ability to restore our communities, our environment, our health and our spirits.

Who are these great business leaders and companies?

- They're people like Andrea Jung and her work with Avon, supporting breast cancer research
- People like Jeffrey Swartz and the extraordinary contribution his company, Timberland, has made through City Year
- People like Susan Knobler and the Gift of Sight program through Lenscrafters (Luxottica)
- People like Oprah Winfrey and her Angel Network
- People like Richard Branson and the generous contribution Virgin is making to the global warming initiative

There are many more, and they're all sending the message that business is embracing the opportunity to restore the planet. Companies are taking up causes and in the process becoming inspiring places to work.

Orenda

It occurred to me that while almost every company wants to give back, and many are giving back in some way, in most cases something's missing. While companies can wipe their brow and say, "OK, we wrote a check to a charity — we gave," and it shows up as a line item on their balance sheet, they know that it's not something their business really stands for. And they know they certainly aren't getting any bang for their philanthropic buck.

I began to wonder: If I could help one business find its soul, were there others out there that could use some help, too? Everyone I consulted cheered me on. And so began Orenda, a strategic corporate philanthropy consulting company. By connecting companies and causes we help businesses integrate their giving program into their corporate culture to create an inspired and inspiring workplace.

I'm often asked where the name came from. While I was formulating the idea of the business I was looking for a word or phrase that meant corporate soul. At that time I was reading Eric Klein and John Izzo's book *Awakening Corporate Soul*. They tell of Native American author Jamake Highwaters and his use of the word *orenda* to describe the tribal soul, or tribal fire. There was the name. The soul of the tribe, the soul of the company — the orenda.

It's so easy and natural to get caught up with hitting sales targets, keeping costs down, reducing headcount and managing growth, but keeping the orenda of your company burning bright is an integral part of your corporate karma.

As I began to talk to business owners and leaders it became apparent that businesses do want to give back in a meaningful way and are seeing an opportunity to create inspired workplaces in the process. But so often the CEOs of small- to medium-sized businesses tell me they don't have the time or human resources to effectively develop strategic philanthropy. It's on their radar, but they just can't manage to get to it. As we all know, however, whatever's important gets done.

I am very excited to have found my purpose, personally and professionally. In fulfilling it, I am helping businesses reach out to benefit the planet and reach into their workplaces to create inspired, motivated employees. As can happen to anyone in business there are moments when I get caught up in the day-to-day operations that demand I turn my focus toward administration and away from my purpose. That's why my morning ritual includes a karma check-in, when I refocus on my mission with clarity.

And on a clear day I can see Africa.

2

Finding Your Emotional Profit Center
The New Corporate Philanthropy

Happiness is when what you think, what you say and what you do are in harmony.
— MOHANDAS GANDHI

John Whitehead, the former chairman of Goldman Sachs, delivers the straight goods regarding corporate philanthropy. He is quoted in James Austin's *The Collaboration Challenge* as saying:

> Don't think that this is some kind of charitable thing where you will get rewarded in heaven. You get rewarded right away because you'll be known as a company that is conscious of its social responsibility; you'll attract better quality employees; your stock will sell at a higher multiple, and all sorts of good things will come of it.

At a recent conference of the Donors Forum of Wisconsin, Timothy J. McClimon, the former CEO of UPS, said he believed all giving, including corporate giving, must come "from the heart."

The former president of General Mills agreed, but then added that *finding* a corporation's heart was the real challenge. We at Orenda believe the challenge is not only finding a company's heart, but rather, finding a company's soul.

Whereas the heart refers to the center of emotion and intuition, the soul is action oriented: a place where, according to one dictionary definition, "thought, action, and emotion" are all bound together. Finding and expressing a company's soul creates much more than positive feelings — it animates and breathes life into a workplace. The company soul is its vital core made manifest. It is the emotional profit center of the company, potentially adding value to the top and bottom line that not only is measurable but also is increasingly critical for long-term business sustainability.

Finding a company's soul requires digging deeper. Where does it live? In its vision and mission statements? In the brand? In its leadership? In the company history? Looking in the right place is key to finding a company's soul and creating a successful corporate philanthropy program.

Looking for Soul in All the Wrong Places

Looking in a Checkbook

Most of us think of giving as generosity with no strings attached. That's how it works in our personal lives. We care about a cause and we make a donation.

In the workplace charitable contributions are often initiated by an employee or leader who has been personally touched by a cause or a non-profit. In many cases it's suppliers and partners who lean on companies to support their worthy cause. In other cases a check is a nice "go away" gift to a particularly persistent non-profit.

Even though checks are written in support of good causes, this kind of philanthropy can be a losing proposition — both for the corporation and the non-profit. For the corporation there may be a heartfelt commitment when the check is signed, but once the non-profit is out of sight, the issue can fade into the background. After all this is a business and there's work to be done. Philanthropy may never find a meaningful place within the company. As time passes and employees change, one non-profit may be dropped and another may benefit. All issues are good issues so it's just a question of which worthy non-profit gets the check in any given year.

Few would argue that check writing is not a good use of a company's resources. The lack of strategy can make these commitments fleeting. There is little opportunity for the company to get behind the cause. It can amount to money being spent with little corporate strategy.

This approach doesn't really serve non-profits well, either. The short-term nature of the gift means that the non-profit is forced to spend valuable time and energy fundraising rather than doing social-change work that impacts lives. Going after small checks year after year takes a lot of resources. And contributions are usually limited to money. There are no volunteers or executive exchanges, no relationships, just a check.

Looking in Marketing

In response to the non-strategic nature of the check-writing approach, philanthropy found a new home in companies' marketing and public relations departments. On the surface the marriage between philanthropy and marketing does make a lot of sense. After all, consumer demand is what has driven the corporate social responsibility movement most dramatically over the last decade.

In a recent Cone survey 86% of Americans said that when price and quality were equal, they would reward companies that support a cause. That's a 30% increase over the previous decade. Companies now regularly publish corporate social responsibility reports and post them on their Websites for all to see. Under the broad strokes of CSR, new accounting practices have emerged, including double bottom line (profits and everything else) and triple bottom line (people, planet, profit). In this sense consumer pressure has been very positive. When setting out to define their philanthropy many companies still undertake extensive surveys among their consumers.

But it may be misguided to ask consumers to define your soul. That would be like asking your friend to determine, based on their understanding of you, who your ideal life partner should be. It may tempting to do so, but it's probably not a good idea.

By its nature marketing is a trend-driven business need reacting to consumer demand. When philanthropy is driven by consumers (or the perception of what consumers want) the result often is relationships that may have sizzle but lack real commitment.

This isn't news to most of us. A survey by the Reputation Institute, commented on in the *Wall Street Journal*, found that "Americans have a general skepticism about philanthropy." No big surprise to those of us who were less than moved when Philip Morris donated money to flood victims or women's education. It's not that these aren't good causes. They are. And they need support. But most of us see this kind of contribution as an attempt to clean up a dirty reputation. We look with suspicion at companies who use their giving to create buzz. It just feels bad.

In *Values Shift* John Izzo, the author and internationally renowned consultant and speaker, best expresses our gut reaction to this kind of advertising. He writes: "The reputational benefits that flow from acts of corporate citizenship depend on their being perceived as genuine acts of citizenship ... Purely altruistic motivation is not required, but the public is impatient with marketing dressed up as citizenship." The point is not that cause marketing is bad. It is a wonderful and natural extension of a company's authentic commitment. It's just that it is ineffective in driving and sustaining a philanthropy program.

Looking for Soul in All the Right Places

Soul Meets Strategy: The New Philanthropy

The new corporate philanthropy is strategic. It partners a business with a relevant cause and integrates the partnership into the corporate culture. It creates an inspirational workplace. It's good for business.

Nobel laureate and economist Milton Friedman influenced a generation to reject corporate philanthropy on the basis that business leaders, as he put it in a *New York Times Magazine* article, had "no responsibilities other than to maximize profits for the shareholders ... the business of business is business." However, as we have seen since, the idea that giving back to communities cannot at the same time bring value to the business is short-sighted. But the idea that marketing dressed up as philanthropy is the only way to create this value is misguided. It's giving from a company's *soul* that makes for good business strategy.

Jim Collins and Jerry Porras's bestseller *Built to Last*, the result of a six-year study of successful businesses, shows a link between the strength of a company's vision and its financial performance. The key to a company's success, according to these authors, is to be "guided by a core ideology — core values and a sense of purpose beyond just making money." The more a company can return to its core (its soul) as the main criterion in its decision-making, the more financially successful it will be. It's a virtuous cycle. The more deeply the company "believes its ideology and consistently lives, breathes and expresses it in all it does," the more successful it will be.

In the winter 2004 edition of *Business Ethics* editor and publisher Marjorie Kelly writes:

> Do socially responsible companies perform better financially? The answer has long been the statistical Holy Grail ... eagerly

sought, ever out of reach. I'm here to announce that search is over. The evidence is in. This is the finding of two meta studies ... 30 years and 112 studies later, it's been proven. Corporate Social Responsibility does go hand in hand with financial out-performance.

Corporate philanthropy as an extension of a company's soul made manifest has the amazing power to drive everything the company does.

Merck

Merck is a powerful example of a visionary company whose philanthropy is the full expression of its values and ideology. Here's how founder George Merck II expresses the ideals that the company lives by today, as quoted in *Built to Last*: "We are workers in industry who are genuinely inspired by the ideals of advancement of medical science and service to humanity."

These ideals were put to the test when Merck developed a drug called Mectizan to treat river blindness (Onchocerciasis), a condition that affects millions of people in the developing world.

In developing the drug Merck assumed that given the widespread nature of the disease, a government or third party would step up to fund its distribution. When no one came forward Merck decided to manufacture and distribute the drug for free. Why? Because it was consistent with the company's ideals. In fact the company's chief executive stated that part of his decision to go forward was to avoid the risk of demoralizing the Merck scientists who had put their hearts into developing the drug.

Based on the research in *Built to Last*, if serving humanity through medical advancement is who you truly are, the more you live up to those ideals, the more financially successful you will become. Taking a stand has helped Merck attract the best scientists and create a culture of innovation that has allowed it to flourish.

Pampered Chef

Pampered Chef (a Berkshire Hathaway company) doesn't just sell useful kitchen tools, it sells a powerful idea. In her book on the company, founder Doris Christopher says she had a vision that she would focus "not on how much money (she) would make, but on how others would benefit." Christopher built a $700-million business by selling essential kitchen tools through a network of saleswomen (called consultants) who perform kitchen shows in people's homes.

Pampered Chef is not only defined by what it does: selling kitchen products. It is also defined, and driven, by its belief in the importance of family mealtime. In fact, the company's stated vision is that "families all around the world should know the joy and rewards of gathering together in the tradition of family mealtimes."

In order to further this core vision, Pampered Chef is a major supporter of Second Harvest in the US and the Canadian Association of Food Banks in Canada. These networks of food banks supply food to soup kitchens, churches and other food relief organizations throughout North America. This commitment puts the company's vision into action: helping those without a sufficient food supply to give their families both the physical and emotional nourishment they need.

Pampered Chef's program with these food banks has raised more than $7 million to date. But it has also raised the spirits of employees who are proud to work for a company that shares their commitment to celebrating the values of family and community.

Creating Inspiring Workplaces

When strategy meets soul, workplaces become inspired. And the need to create inspired workplaces has never been more pressing. With baby boomers retiring at record rates it will be more and more difficult for companies to attract skilled talent. One clue to this shift is the sheer number of business publications with dedicated Best Places to Work issues. Understanding how to attract, retain and motivate skilled workers is more critical than ever.

According to the Irish author, philosopher and management guru Charles Handy, in *The Hungry Spirit: Beyond Capitalism*, there are three parts to our soul: the sense of making a difference (purpose), a feeling of responsibility for others (compassion and social justice) and the satisfaction of living a life that is true to one's real values (congruence). Creating an emotional profit center in the workplace, then, allows the soul of the company to meet those three needs and inspire the workforce.

The role of the employer has changed because of other fundamental changes in society. People used to connect to their life values through family, church and community. People expected problems to be solved by church, community and government. All of these roles have shifted. The family structure has changed. The role of church and religion had declined. The expectation of "community" has all but disappeared. And government, well, what's happened could be the subject of a whole other book. As a result of all this, business leaders are now expected to play societal roles.

Mark Sarner, president of Manifest Communications, Canada's leading social marketing agency, told Orenda in a recent interview: "People are walking around in a values vacuum, with a hole in their hearts. They need to be connected and engaged." The workplace, even though it is fundamentally a community of strangers, represents the only sense of community for many people. The challenge employers face is to create an environment with common bonds to keep employees connected. As Sarner put it:

> People are looking for hope and engagement. Hope that things can be better, for them and for the world, and engagement in some way in making things better. A "cause" that is relevant

to the business has the potential to be binding and animating, creating an alignment between the company and the employees.

In the talent pool, which is evaporating, employers cannot compete on compensation, benefits or the business model. Everyone can offer the same thing. Sarner added: "The one distinguishing factor from company to company will be the '*values*-added' proposition." Consider some statistics:

- 72 percent of employed Americans would choose to work for a company that supports charitable causes when deciding between two jobs with the same location, responsibilities, pay and benefits. The response rate climbs to 87 percent for employed students over the age of 18 (Deloitte 2004)
- More than half of surveyed MBA students indicated they would accept a lower salary in order to work for a socially responsible company (Net ImpactSurvey: New Leaders, New Perspectives, 2006)
- When one thousand working adults were asked whether they would rather earn high salaries or earn "enough" doing work that makes the world a better place, 86% chose the latter — a steep increase from 10 years earlier (Universum)
- 81% of Americans consider a company's social commitment when deciding where to work (Cone 2004)

In his book *Inspire!* Lance Secretan writes that

individuals and teams who are inspired and enthused are operating on a different plane than the rest of us, and they know it and cherish it. People frequently move from well-paying positions where they are highly motivated, to lesser paying positions where they are inspired.

People are inspired by connection and engagement, which create a sense of purpose. In the old paradigm reward fuels performance. In the new paradigm purpose fuels performance.

The valuable experiences of companies that have successfully embedded philanthropy programs into the workplace are threaded throughout this book. These are companies that not only support a cause but also get their entire company engaged in the issue. Employees come to care deeply about an issue and roll up their sleeves, do executive exchanges, take overseas expeditions, sit on boards and provide in-kind donations. With each act of generosity they feel greater and greater pride in, and connection to, the place where they work. They value their work life beyond a paycheck and a balance sheet. They have discovered an emotional profit center in the work they do.

Some of the organizations are Fortune 500 companies like Avon, LensCrafters and Timberland. Others are small giants like Robert Kent Photography, Spectrum Health Care and Zingerman's Delicatessen. Some are public, others private. All, however, are attuned to the transformational power of good corporate karma.

The CEOs we feature in this book echo one clear sentiment. They say that it's important to make giving strategic and the results clear, but they emphasize that when the whole company becomes inspired by giving back, corporate philanthropy "comes around" to create positive personal and business results. Whether it's in the form of loyalty and retention, innovation, trust in leadership and sense of camaraderie, giving back comes around to create incredible results. And as you'll continue to see throughout this book, this faith is not misplaced. Companies that have taken the lead in embracing the new philanthropy have experienced good corporate karma firsthand.

Here's how Michael E. Porter and Mark R. Kramer put it in the *Harvard Business Review* of December 2002: "When corporations support the right causes in the right ways — when they get the where and the how right — they set in motion a virtuous cycle ... both the corporations and the causes they support reap important benefits. "

PART 2

How to Give Together

(3)

Step #1
Lead with Inspiration

If you give money, spend yourself with it.
— HENRY THOREAU

Great leaders breathe life and spirit into their organizations. They inspire others.

Companies led by inspiring leaders create environments that attract good people and make them want to stick around. Inspirational business leaders know how to appeal to people's hearts and souls, giving them reason to come to work beyond simply working for a paycheck. They stir passion and purpose in their people.

The Speed of the Leader Is the Speed of the Pack

Years ago, when I was building my first business with her, I was taught by my lifelong friend and mentor Tricia Secretan of the Secretan Center that the "speed of the leader is the speed of the pack." It is a leadership concept that has shown up for me over and over again in my life.

Many of us have been fortunate enough to experience great business leaders on our personal journeys. Much has been written about great leadership, and it's clear that an essential ingredient is a connection to community and an emotional tie to making a difference. Inspirational leaders hold the moral and ethical compass for the company. They don't just talk the talk, they walk the walk of their company's values. They question, deepen and enrich conventional leadership thinking.

"Leadership is a serving relationship with others that inspires their growth and makes the world a better place," Lance Secretan writes in *Inspire!* He goes on to describe inspirational leaders as "Higher Ground" leaders. These leaders, he says, understand *why* they're here, *what* they stand for and *how* they'll serve. When a corporate leader brings that sense of *being* as well as *doing* to the corporate table, a spirit of inspiration whispers through the company.

When employees observe their president/CEO engaged and committed to a community partnership the program becomes more relevant, inspiring and attractive. The leader's behavior sends a message of caring about more than profits. It sends a message of caring about humanity. It builds trust.

And trust is of supreme importance. In a recent article in *Canadian Business* Graham Lowe of the Great Place to Work Institute, a global workplace consulting firm that compiles best-workplaces lists in 29 countries, says its research shows that trust is the bedrock of a positive organizational culture. Employees trust managers who are concerned about their well-being, listen and respond to their input, are open and honest about change and consistently model the organization's values in their own actions.

Great Leaders Lead by Example

Here's a compelling lesson in leading by example from the life of Gandhi.

A grandmother once brought her grandson to Gandhi. The boy, it seemed, had an insatiable appetite for sugar that was threatening his health.

"Please," the grandmother pleaded with Gandhi, "tell him to stop eating sugar. He has so much respect for you. He will listen to what you say."

"Please go away and come back in four days," replied Gandhi.

The woman and her grandson did as requested. When they returned Gandhi looked into the boy's eyes and said, "Stop eating sugar ... it will harm your body."

After a short silence the grandmother asked, "Sir, why did you ask us to wait four days before speaking to my grandson?"

"Madame," Gandhi replied, "four days ago I myself had not stopped eating sugar."

If the purpose of a great philanthropy program is to breathe spirit into the corporate culture by engaging employees, then the leader's most important role is to carry the torch by rolling up their sleeves and getting involved. People will follow.

A corporate philanthropy program usually begins for one of the following reasons:

- The CEO spearheads it, knowing that it is a good and smart thing to do
- The CEO has a personal connection to a cause and sees an opportunity for the company to help
- The founder/owner has reached a stage where they feel business is good and it's time to do something to leave a legacy
- An employee or group of employees brings an idea to management and they say, "Sure, let's do it"
- HR comes up with an idea and sends out a memo to gather support

Whatever the catalyst, the messenger, the champion, the person carrying the torch should be the leader of the company. Not the HR department. Not the VP of something who has been instructed to do it.

Why? Because CEO involvement sends the message that the cause is strategically important to the company.

Dr. Myron Wentz and USANA Health Sciences

Dr. Myron Wentz, chairman and CEO of USANA Health Sciences, gave me one of those "Is it really necessary?" looks when I first asked him to participate in an expedition to El Salvador to visit the villages that we were supplying with nutritional supplements for children. When I told him it was he agreed to go. The project began to weave its way into USANA's core purpose when we returned from that trip and shared with others in the company film footage of Dr. Wentz in the medical centers and orphanages where USANA's products were being distributed, sitting cross-legged on the dirt floor, holding young children while connecting with their mothers, village elders and health-care workers.

Subsequent to that trip similar trips were taken to Mexico, Eastern Europe — including Romania and the Ukraine — and finally to Uganda. Each year Dr. Wentz became more committed, inspired and engaged. This became apparent to more and more USANA constituents as we traveled the world to interact with them at regular corporate meetings. Seeing the authenticity of his involvement connected them to him and the company, creating an emotional profit center for the company. It would not have happened to nearly the same extent had someone other than Dr. Wentz been the one championing the cause.

Jeffrey Swartz and Timberland

Jeffrey Swartz is the third generation of the Swartz family to run Timberland. He loved the business he grew up with. But when he took the reins he knew he was going to bring something different to the company. In a serendipitous moment Swartz found himself in a meeting with the executive director of the fledging non-profit City Year, who took it upon himself to show Swartz how shoes and boots could change the world. What began as a small donation of 50 pairs of boots and Swartz's personal commitment to four hours a week of volunteer work transformed him and the entire company.

Swartz was astonished when his volunteer work put him face to face with people struggling to overcome personal hardships who were right around the corner from his own office in New Hampshire. He was determined to make the experience of serving available to all of Timberland's employees.

In 1992 Swartz spearheaded the Path of Service™ program, which offered Timberland employees 16 hours of paid leave for community service each year. In 1995, when Timberland was facing dwindling profits, he refused to follow his bankers' suggestion to cut the program. Instead Swartz stepped up and doubled the amount of employee volunteer hours. Today employees receive 40 hours of paid time off per year to serve their communities, and the program has also inspired a longer-term "service sabbatical." Sabbatical recipients are given up to six months' leave of absence to volunteer full time at a non-profit organization.

Swartz's commitment has transformed the lives of Timberland employees who have, together, logged over 250,000 hours of volunteer service since the program's inception. It has also made Timberland one of the most socially responsible corporations in the world.

Management Matters

Although it's up to leaders to champion the cause, they must also ensure that the management team is on board from the outset.

Strong leaders know how to ensure that the right people are

included and consulted in important business decisions. Including others in the decision will prevent the resentment and resistance that can occur when decisions are imposed on people who have not been part of the decision-making process.

As Tricia Secretan, vice president of the Secretan Center, puts it, "People support that which they help to create."

A company's management team should be on the front line of establishing the company's philanthropy program. Include your team in choosing the appropriate cause category and charitable partner(s). Make sure they are integrally involved in embedding the program into the culture of the company.

This is why we at Orenda, before signing a contract with a corporate client to design, develop and implement their philanthropy program, recommend that we first meet with the entire management team — we want to ensure that they are supportive of the idea of a philanthropy initiative. We then request that they become part of the analysis process to decide what type of cause the company should support, and that they help select the charitable/non-profit organization that the company will partner with. Their inclusion in the process makes it so much more likely that they will engage with the project and get their own departments behind it. They may eventually delegate someone else from their department to be the go-to person for them, but by then everyone will know of their ongoing support.

Spectrum Health Care

At Spectrum Health Care the entire senior management team was invited to a presentation on strategic corporate philanthropy. At the end of the presentation Lori Lord, the COO and champion of the program, asked for candid feedback. It was evident that this management team was comfortable being candid. At the end of the meeting, after questions were asked and answered, she asked who would support the integration of a philanthropy program into the company. The response was unanimous. Before the meeting was adjourned an off-site meeting of the entire management team was planned to decide which type of cause made the most sense and to determine the objectives of the program.

The next step, after the off-site meeting, was to reassemble the team to look at three different humanitarian organizations that met the criteria they had agreed on. The management team thus had the opportunity to be part of the selection process. By the time the choice had been made they had fully engaged with the program. They then agreed that a committee should be assembled to move the project forward.

Assembling a Team

Like most other initiatives a philanthropy program needs support and input from many internal departments, and effective communication is critical. We usually suggest that companies assemble a focused team or committee to ensure that each essential department is able to provide input and functional support.

Who should be represented on the team? Here are some suggestions:

- President/CEO, to carry the torch and deliver the message
- Finance, to collect and distribute donations, keep track of who is contributing and allocate expenses related to the project to the correct accounting code
- Legal, to work with finance on technical aspects of the type of giving program, determine whether the company needs a Foundation and set up the tax structure of the initiative
- Sales/Marketing, to brand the initiative, make sure the message is communicated to the sales force and decide whether to include it in marketing materials
- Event Planner, because events are the most effective and direct

way to deliver the message of the philanthropy project and inspire employees to support it. Whether at a quarterly sales meeting, an annual convention or regional off-site meetings, getting in front of employees with visual emotional communication and giving them some ownership of the program is the single most significant method of creating an emotional profit center

- Information Technology, to set up and track contribution methods as well as keep the Website current
- Communications, to develop and design ongoing communication from the very inception of the program, with a schedule of regular progress reports
- Public Relations, to spread the news beyond the company and respond to customer and media inquiries
- Human Resources, to ensure that all new employees are made aware of the program during orientation
- Operations (Manufacturing/Purchasing/ Research and Development), if a product is being developed and/or contributed
- Customer Service, if the initiative is being extended out to customers
- A Cause Representative from the non-profit or charity for input and feedback
- Regional office representative(s), because if a company has more than one corporate office or location it's important that each group be part of the planning. Regional offices or locations are often given some autonomy to create their own program linked to the corporate program by a common cause. However, the more involved they are with the development of the core cause program, the more consistent the program will be
- Point person (project manager), to take charge of moving the initiative forward. It could be one of the people listed above, or another individual who is able to commit the time and

resources necessary and has the ability to hold others accountable for their roles

By committing to a monthly check-in from this team the project will be assimilated into the function of each department, and the process will flow from there.

The Corporate Giving Statement

One of the most important early steps for the team is to craft a statement that will create the parameters of the giving program. This statement may include:

- Why you're giving (your purpose)
- Who you're giving to (one charity, foundation, category, locally or internationally)
- What you're giving (money, time, in-kind resources)
- When you're giving it (monthly, annually, event driven)
- And how you're giving (employee programs, corporate matches, volunteer time)

This statement will help:

- The company respond to the requests it receives
- Increase awareness of company giving among employees, customers and the community
- Prevent well-intentioned but misguided corporate funding of inappropriate organizations or people
- Sustain commitment even in times of corporate change

The rest of this part of the book walks you through ways to design your company's giving statement, as well as a year-long action plan and budget.

LEADERSHIP CHECKLIST

1. *The philanthropy message comes from the president/CEO*
2. *The management team is part of the creation of the program*
3. *A team is assembled to drive the program*
4. *Prepare to craft a Corporate Giving Statement, action plan and budget*

(4)

Step #2
Connect Company and Cause

We must use time wisely and forever realize
that the time is always ripe to do right.
— NELSON MANDELA

Most often, businesses write checks to the CEO's favorite charity or the non-profits on whose boards they or their friends sit. Sometimes the check goes to the most recent organization to have called for a donation. There's usually no plan, never mind a strategy. Sometimes this works, where there's a serendipitous fit between company and charity or cause. Most times it doesn't. Management is perplexed why so few of their employees show up for the golf tournament or silent auction fundraisers they've organized. It should be obvious to them that anyone who feels obligated to give time or money to their pet cause is going to grumble every step of the way.

Relevance and Cause

Businesses who contribute in this way are missing the boat. They should know that given any encouragement most people will come to work not only to earn a paycheck but also to make a contribution to the mission of the company and make good on opportunities to learn and grow and be recognized for their accomplishments. People are looking for a sense of community at work. Any initiative that allows community to be created in the workplace can provide great value.

The day-to-day activities of employees in the workplace are directly related to moving the purpose of the business forward. These activities are what binds the person at the front desk to the shipping department to the boardroom. By connecting your company to a relevant cause you will strengthen these bonds and create engagement, giving employees a sense of purpose beyond the business itself.

What does your business stand for and where is the social need that fits what you stand for? How do you identify the best cause for your business? How do you sift through the hundreds of thousands of non-profits out there to find one that has what it takes to show up as a great long-term partner?

Your philanthropy program will create the strongest bond if it is an extension of your company values — if it becomes an integral part of the business, creating an emotional profit center.

In contrast, if there is no real fit between what you do as a business and the cause you are supporting, the connection will be lost. Let's say you're in the design/construction business. The purpose of your company is to provide safe and inspiring environments for people to live and work in. Your CEO's pet cause, meanwhile, is funding breast cancer. This is a recipe for apathy when it comes to making the connection to a cause and creating synergy between company and cause. Your people are not going to link arms and mobilize the way they would for something related to the what or why of their work.

If you're in business you've identified why you're in business and how your product or service is improving the quality of life for your customer. Now extend that beyond your balance sheet and identify a connection to a social need or cause that could also benefit. Every business can find a socially relevant cause. Perhaps:

- The product/service you make your living from is greatly needed in underdeveloped areas. Focusing on what they know best, LensCrafters has developed the Gift of Sight Program. Since 1988 they have provided free eye exams and glasses to over three million people in need
- Your product or service could be given to an existing non-profit to impact the work they do. Ericsson has established a network within the United Nations and International Federation of Red Cross and Red Crescent Societies. Ericsson Response provides immediate emergency telecommunications service in disaster relief
- Specific talent in your company could collectively make a huge difference. Through the M·A·C (Cosmetics) Good Spirits program, M·A·C makeup artists offer one-on-one support to those living with HIV/AIDS, teaching them how to use makeup to enhance their appearance and minimize problems resulting from the illness or medication
- The clients you serve have a collective challenge that needs support. As the "company for women" Avon provides not just beauty products but also an entrepreneurial program for women to enhance their financial, physical and emotional wellness. In response to the needs of women and their families the Avon Breast Cancer Crusade for more than a decade has raised funds and awareness for advancing access to care and finding a cure for breast cancer. From 1992 through 2005 the Avon Breast Cancer Crusade has raised and donated more than $400 million in 50 countries worldwide for medical

research, access to treatment, screening, support services and education. Avon's Breast Cancer Crusade is relevant to their sales representatives and customers alike

The closer your company mission, calling and purpose are to that of your charity partner, the more smoothly the project will be integrated into your corporate culture. A perfect example of this is the common theme in the tag lines of Timberland and its partner City Year. Timberland's is, "Make It Better." City Year's is, "Young enough to want to change the world and old enough to do it."

And consider Hasbro. In the day-to-day business of "doing business" it is easy to lose touch with the importance of *play* and what it really means to a child's life. Hasbro's philanthropy programs, however, are specifically designed to keep the power of play front of mind. It is in the business of bringing smiles to children's lives. It was the first corporate sponsor to help spearhead the creation of Boundless Playgrounds, a non-profit that creates playground access for children of all abilities. These unique playgrounds give children, with and without disabilities, the ability to develop essential skills for life as they learn together through play.

When making a decision about the cause category that's best for your business, think long term. Changing from cause to cause will prevent the initiative from taking root in your organization. You may contribute over time to a variety of non-profit organizations within a cause category, but stay focused on a theme.

Cause Categories

What business are you in? What do you stand for? What are your corporate values? What causes are relevant to your business? What causes do your customers care about? Which ones do your employees care about? Where's the social need that may be aligned with the answers to those questions? Finding a cause that is relevant to the business you are in may be the most important strategy for ensuring the success of your philanthropy initiative.

Philanthropy is about finding solutions for meeting the needs and ending the suffering of the planet, of people, of all creatures great and small. Causes generally fall into one of seven categories:

1. Economic Development
2. Education
3. Environment
4. Gender
5. Health
6. Human Rights
7. Technology

Once you have identified a cause category the next step is to determine the scope of your philanthropy program. You need to decide whether your initiative will contribute to a single non-profit or multiple non-profits that work for the cause and whether your reach will be local or global in scope.

Focus: One or More?

Many of the clients we talk to at Orenda have brought us on board because although they've been giving, they haven't been doing so through a focused strategy. It's been one thing this quarter, something else next quarter, with no identity or consistency to their giving program.

It is critical for you to decide what you're going to support. It needs to be strategic, reflecting who you are and what you stand for and thus becoming a touchstone for your employees. In the branding world, success is measured by the ability to boil a product or service down to one idea. The same applies to your philanthropy program. Your employees need to be able to say, "Yes, we support *x*." If your program stands for too many ideas or issues its impact will be diluted. You may choose one charity partner, or as Avon has done with breast cancer, you may give support to a number of various organizations all committed to the same cause.

Your decision about whether to select one or more partners should be guided by the scope of your giving. If you are a small business with a few employees you'll probably create more synergy by selecting one charity or non-profit to support. This will help you avoid spreading yourself too thin.

Many companies that we talked to express concern that choosing one charity could create resentment in their workforce. They are worried that employees will feel pressured to contribute — that they might even fear that not doing so could affect their performance reviews. Other companies say they fear some employees might be reluctant to contribute because they are already contributing time and money to personal causes. In response to this concern some companies have developed "matching" programs in which the company matches employee donations or gives them paid time off to volunteer at the charities or causes of their choice.

Companies who make this their only approach to philanthropy face a challenge when it comes to creating leverage and synergy. The giving is so diffuse that the "connection" that people crave is not made. Our experience shows the benefits of a company being patient with its program. When they introduce it and let the results gradually spread through the organization rather than imposing it on people, the results are extraordinary. The first year after the Children's Hunger Fund™ initiative was introduced at USANA total contributions were about $120,000. By the third year they were over $1 million. The program was not imposed on anyone. It grew organically as people started sharing their experiences.

Local or Global Reach?

Determining whether your efforts should be directed to a local or international project is both a strategic and individual decision. Many companies are committed to making a difference in their own backyards, while others see contributing their efforts to the developing world as more compelling and appropriate.

Zingerman's Delicatessen started out as a small specialty shop in Ann Arbor, Michigan, and has grown to become the Zingerman's Community of Businesses (ZCOB) — eight different businesses, each with its own specialty and all within the Ann Arbor area. When ZCOB was deciding how to give back they knew they wanted their initiative to be local and relevant. They started Food Gatherers in 1988, a non-profit with a clear mission to "rescue" food and distribute it in their area. In its first year it rescued and redistributed 86,000 pounds of food. Now, nearly two decades later, the amount is two to three tons *per day*. By 1997 Food Gatherers had grown to provide a range of services to the homeless.

The importance of staying local has not been lost on the ownership of Zingerman's. "It would be a very different community if we didn't do it," Paul Saginaw says.

When Orenda was working with the management team at Spectrum Health Care, a company that provides home-based health-care services in Toronto, Canada, it became clear to us that health care would be the cause that would be embraced. It was a strategic fit. The question became whether the company should focus on a local or international initiative.

We took a look at need and concluded that with socialized medical care in Canada, most Canadians had access to care at some level. There were, however, millions of people in the developing world who didn't even have access to clean drinking water, a prerequisite to all things health related. It didn't take long for the management team to unanimously decide to look for an opportunity in a developing nation. Spectrum adopted the village of Xalibe (*shall-ee-bay*) in central Guatemala and developed an ongoing program for improving the quality of health care in the village, starting with clean water.

Vancity is Canada's largest credit union. Its 46 branches are all located in beautiful British Columbia. In determining how best to focus its philanthropic dollars, Vancity decided to focus on its strengths, providing financial grants and awards to create strong non-profits and social enterprises throughout the province. From grants to create more after-school programming for kids in Port Coquitlam to supporting an organization working to increase the employability of people with developmental disabilities in Burnaby, Vancity's financial support is impacting lives on a local level.

Once you've identified the *what* (your cause) and the *where* (your focus area) it's time to look for the *who* (the best charity or partners for your company).

Sifting for the Right Partner

There are well over one million registered non-profit organizations in North America. Generally they fall into one of the categories mentioned above. Sifting through them to find the one(s) that fit your company and meet the criteria you're looking for can be overwhelming. Perhaps you won't have to sift, though. Non-profits are always looking for funding and have figured out that corporations are starting to step up to the plate for relevant causes. A number of them may come looking for you.

Here are the criteria to consider in choosing the right philanthropy initiative:

- Chemistry
- Financial responsibility

- Hands-on opportunities
- Faith and religion
- Sustainability
- Exclusivity
- Administrative capabilities
- Structure for giving

Let's look at each one of these in detail.

Chemistry

A good rule of thumb is the smaller the company, the smaller the charity should be. A small business will get lost in the politics of large non-profits, whereas a small charity founded by someone still passionate about the cause is usually a great fit for a business with a small management team and employee base.

One of Orenda's smaller clients is a good example of a mismatch. It had been contributing to a large national non-profit whose central offices were in the same city. But as we quickly saw when the company asked us to project-manage the initiative, it was the wrong fit. Our client's contributions were small compared with other corporations giving to the non-profit. It was always someone different from the non-profit who showed up to our meetings. A partnership between a business and a non-profit requires equal commitment from both sides. (In chapter 9 we will discuss how good charity partners always "show up.")

Great partnerships involve great chemistry between the leaders of both the company and the non-profit. As in any relationship, the chemistry can grow over time, but there's usually some connection right from the start. I met Dave Phillips, president of Children's Hunger Fund™, at LAX airport as we were boarding a plane to fly to San Salvador. From our many previous telephone conversations I had sensed that this was a man with a vision. More than that, a vision that was synergistic with the purpose and passion of Dr. Myron Wentz, my boss at USANA Health Sciences. It was going to be a good partnership.

I didn't have the experience at the time to know the importance of that initial connection to the long-term success of the partnership. It did become apparent to me over the next few years as we traveled the developing world together and I watched a friendship grow between Dave and Dr. Wentz that bonds USANA to Children's Hunger Fund™ to this day. Dave contributes monthly to the USANA newsletter, attends every event to deliver an update from center stage and makes himself available when asked to participate in USANA activities.

Timberland's work with City Year is the ultimate example of a partnership that has grown into a true collaboration. Through its Youth Service Corps, City Year engages youth aged 17 to 24 in 10 months of community service and leadership development. How did this partnership come about? When a cofounder of City Year met with two company executives to thank them for their initial donation of boots and shoes, both realized that they shared a common goal of strengthening communities.

"The meeting was important," recalls Timberland's former marketing vice president Ken Frietas, "because for the first time we realized there was more here than a typical charitable contribution. There was a real connection. The similarities between what each organization wanted to do and how it planned to achieve its vision were striking."

The Timberland/City Year connection is not just about donating money and product — it's also about each enterprise offering value to the other.

Many people in the non-profit world have spent so much of their time fundraising that they may not necessarily have developed the awareness of the need for truly showing up in a partnership. They need to be prepared to do more than receive the check. They need to be prepared to step up and be part of the corporate philanthropic initiative.

When asked about corporate partnership, Dave Phillips of Children's Hunger Fund™ told us:

> Ultimately, success comes down to approaching a partnership with the needs of the corporate partner being addressed. It can't just be about the charity's need for support. Corporations are concerned about their image, public relations, market share, sales volume, employee involvement and a spirit of giving back to the community. As charities we are challenged to find ways to incorporate these needs when crafting strategic partnerships.

It's also important to be sure that the contribution you want to make is something the charity wants, needs and can accept. One of our clients has a protein supplement they wanted their employees to be able to purchase and donate to the local children's charity. It turned out that the children in the facility were considered wards of the state and the regulations prevented the non-profit from giving nutritional supplements to them — something we were not made aware of until after the commitment had been made. A simple letter of agreement outlining the expectations of both the company and the non-profit is valuable in managing expectations.

Emily Franson, director of Community Outreach for Choice Humanitarian, says that from the non-profit perspective there are three criteria that will help the partnership from the very beginning:

1. Striking the right partnership with the key players and getting buy-in across the company
2. Finding the balance. Because it's a partnership and you want them to buy into it, the initial conversations must be fluid and collaborative
3. Using a memorandum of understanding or some other type of

agreement to outline what each party is expecting. This really helps clear up any potential misunderstandings and is useful to refer to as the project develops

To create inspiration in the workplace, companies need a cause partner that is going to be a full partner. And vice versa. A charity looking for long-term funding and engagement must be aware that simple check writing is a thing of the past. Collaboration and partnership define the new philanthropy. As Lynne Twist writes in her book *The Soul of Money*:

> There is no way that rich people (corporations) can really change anything with money without the passion and commitment of partners who know how to do what needs to be done. It is only when that on-site wisdom is valued, honored and embraced in partnership that lasting gains are made. Absent the commitment to confront the challenges we face together as a human community, charity doesn't solve problems. It separates us from the problem temporarily and gets us off the hook. Our societies have trained us to give and accept help, when in fact, what is needed is full engagement, collaboration and partnership.

Financial Responsibility

Financial responsibility is the "show me the money" factor. In the non-profit sector transparent reporting and guidelines have gone far in ensuring that money gets where it's supposed to go. However, it's important for you and your constituents to feel confident that this is the case.

There are watchdogs for the non-profit world. Some of these groups (listed below) rank charities with a star rating like the movies, and one of the things they're looking for is financial responsibility.

As a rule at least 80% of a charity's funding should go directly into their programs, with 20% or less used for administration and fundraising.

At Orenda our benchmark is 85%. We look for partners for our clients who are operating on 15% or less.

Millennium Promise is a non-profit dedicated to working toward the millennium development goals of eliminating extreme poverty by 2025, village by village. This non-profit dedicates 100% of a corporate partner's funding to the specific village interventions the corporation has come on board to support, while raising funds for their own overhead through other channels.

By law and governance, charities and non-profits are required to be financially transparent. Their financial statements must be available to the public and generally can be found on their Websites.

Here are some excellent resources to help you do some due diligence on a specific charity:

- For those registered in the US: www.charitynavigator.org and www.guidestar.org
- Although Canada does not have the same watchdog agencies, Imagine Canada provides information on Canadian non-profits (www.nonprofitscan.ca)

Hands-on Opportunities

Depending on your cause and the nature of the giving you may be looking for an opportunity to participate in ways other than or in addition to funding. Your people are more likely to catch the heartbeat of giving by rolling up their sleeves and getting up close and personal with need. Consider the difference in inspirational impact between:

- Contributing cash through a payroll deduction to Habitat for Humanity and getting out and swinging a hammer to build a home for someone in need

- Paying a fee to enter a golf tournament to raise money for Evergreen and getting out there to plant trees in a schoolyard, creating some shade in an otherwise concrete playground for a group of inner-city students

Hands-on opportunities are where inspiration dwells. Look for a partner that either has a program in place or is willing to work with you to create an opportunity for your employees to get personally engaged.

A few cautions are in order.

Unfortunately some non-profits are unable to provide the type of hands-on opportunities that many employees wish for. Perhaps the work is being done with people who need anonymity (abused children or women, for example). Creative thinking will help uncover some ways to help. Walls can be painted, skills can be offered to the non-profit from the corporate skill bank, fundraisers can be hosted and so on. There's always something that can be done.

Also, having a large of group of well-intentioned foreigners show up in a village in the developing world has proven counter-productive in some cases. However, if the infrastructure is in place so the corporate group can work alongside and *with* the villagers, it can work. The mistake is in thinking that we should be doing something *for* them. How many stories are there of wells dug by well-meaning humanitarians only to become unusable because no one local was trained to maintain them? In our zeal to give back we sometimes forget that the work of many of these great non-profits is designed to create sustainable development independent of outside involvement.

As Jeff Flug, CEO of Millennium Promise, pointed out in an interview with Orenda:

> We have partnered with district, regional and national govern-ments to help develop the resources necessary to help these

people get on the first rung of the ladder out of extreme poverty. We're showing them that they can do it on their own. We're happy to take a group from the company to visit the village they are supporting, but it's not a "roll up your sleeves and get to work" kind of trip. The villagers are proud of the work they're doing on their own. To show their immense gratitude, they will extend their hospitality with a celebratory welcome, but even that takes them away from the important work they are doing.

Faith and Religion

Historically charity has its roots in religion. The value of compassion is spoken of in religious communities more than anywhere else. Most non-profits and charities are associated with organized religion and founded on the doctrine of that religion. Thank God, Allah, Buddha, the Universe and all the other names associated with spiritual guidance that organized religion has sprung from for all the good work these groups are doing. However, the multicultural fabric of our communities and workplaces does require sensitivity and understanding regarding the nature of faith-based charitable organizations.

In a program I helped a client with when I was still very early in my learning curve, the question of faith-based vs. non-faith-based non-profits didn't even occur to me. I found an organization that was doing extraordinary humanitarian work relevant to the client's business. Everything else that seemed important was there: great chemistry with the founder of the charity, financial responsibility, exciting opportunities for my client to truly engage their workforce and hands-on participation opportunities for the employees. It seemed a perfect fit.

Upon launching the first project with this group, however, I discovered that the charity had been founded by a devout evangelical Christian, and the whole organization was built on the doctrine of his church. Every activity, every day of every project was undertaken with an evangelical theme. My corporate client, meanwhile, had a very diverse employee profile. Most people were either of that faith themselves and thrilled or not of that faith and tolerant. But I quickly began to hear rumblings, as well as direct feedback, that others were offended and were refusing to participate.

However, the program was otherwise so well received and such a good fit for the company that we ended up developing a protocol that informed everyone before they committed to an individual project within the program that this was a Christian group. We asked them to sign a waiver indicating that they were aware of this and that the company's involvement with the charity in no way reflected the beliefs of the company. Valuing the partnership so much, the director of the charity also agreed that they would be as discreet as possible, without sacrificing their own values. It all worked out.

The key is to understand that much of the charity and humanitarian work being done today will have a spiritual element to it. Determine whether this is an issue for your business and build the appropriate due diligence into your search for the best partner.

Sustainability

Here's a well-known proverb, but with a twist: "Give a man a fish, you feed him for a day; teach a man to fish, you feed him for a lifetime; teach a man to teach a man to fish, you feed a village."

Most charities and causes today are working toward sustainability for those they serve. "If you are coming to help me, you are wasting your time," an indigenous peoples saying goes. "But if you are coming because your liberation is bound up with mine, then let us work together."

Relief work that provides immediate aid in crisis situations is important. The opportunity to contribute support during these times is, of course, extremely valuable. However, in setting up a long-term program, partner your company with an organization looking to provide sustainability to the people they serve. This will help your program to be part of the solution on an ongoing basis and to celebrate progress.

If your cause is to counter homelessness, look for an organization like the Doe Fund. Their belief statement reads:

> We believe that every human being has the potential to be a productive, contributing member of society. What some lack is the opportunity. The Doe Fund is a non-profit organization that empowers people to break the cycle of homelessness, welfare dependency and incarceration through innovative paid work programs, housing support services and business ventures.

That's not to say that relief agencies aren't a vital part of the fabric of charity. They are — the soup kitchen and the homeless shelter make a difference.

From the perspective of corporate initiative, when employees see progress and results that lead to sustainability, long-term commitment to the project grows.

Exclusivity: Other Corporate Partners?

It's important for you, in researching a potential charitable partner, to review other corporate donors to that charity. There may be a conflict between funders.

It's not unusual for companies to seek category exclusivity. In fact too often companies walk away from charitable partners to maintain exclusivity. Because of this competitive thinking companies miss out on bringing different but synergistic skills to the table. It's a pity because this kind of collaboration could strengthen relationships between competitors in the same industry and give a boost to their networking efforts.

And in any case if the giving is truly genuine, it probably should not matter who else is giving to the charity. I heard a story about a children's hospital that had begun a large capital campaign. One of their biggest contributors was a regional telecommunications company. A hospital foundation board member came to the table with a significant contribution from another telecommunications company, whose board he also sat on. The original telecom contributor threatened to pull its funding if the hospital foundation accepted the contribution from its competitor. The question, of course, is, "What about the children? Isn't it about the children?" I understand where this corporation's thinking comes from: the old philanthropy of check writing for the purpose of public relations and marketing.

Administrative Capabilities

If employees and other constituents wish to make contributions, make sure your charity partner is able and willing to issue tax receipts. (This is not necessary if you have a company foundation with charitable status, which will be discussed below.) We encourage our corporate clients to keep a spreadsheet of employee names and contact information, along with the cumulative contributions they've made, and send it to the charity annually for it to issue receipts directly.

Structure for Giving

There are two fundamentally different structures for your philanthropy program:

1. A direct-giving program (supporting one or several charities, or a community foundation)
2. A company-sponsored foundation (supporting several charities with a grant program)

Direct-giving program

This is by far the simpler form. A company donates cash (both corporate and employee contributions) and accounts for all other forms of contribution directly to a charity or a community foundation and on its own balance sheet. We usually recommend that our clients begin with this system until their contributions are large enough and their reach is wide enough that they are open to accepting grant applications from a number of non-profits for support.

Company-sponsored foundation

Many companies prefer to establish a corporate foundation. A corporate foundation is an independent grant-making body. It's a separate legal entity and may be registered as its own tax-exempt charitable organization.

Corporate foundations come in many shapes and sizes, and their funding may come from a variety of sources. For example, corporations may:

- Start a foundation with a substantial endowment, using its earnings to contribute to a cause
- Make periodic contributions from profits and/or employee contributions
- Develop a combination of both methods

Foundations are appropriate where companies want to address the root causes of significant issues that threaten the health of communities and thereby the health of the corporations themselves (e.g., Avon). The structure of foundations makes them ideal for giving to more recipients over a longer period of time. Also the structure of foundations makes them preferable when a company contributes to many charitable organizations rather than focusing on a single charitable beneficiary.

Here are several specific benefits to establishing a corporate foundation:

- If a corporate foundation also has charitable status it can issue its own tax receipts. So, for example, if the corporation has an employee contribution program, the foundation can issue its own tax receipts rather than relying on the non-profit to supply them
- All foundations must have a board. In the case of corporate foundations these generally involve the CEO and senior executives but may also include employees from all parts of the company. This is a steering committee that is ready-made to secure employee engagement and loyalty
- The purpose of the foundation must be outlined in its charter, thus providing strategic focus to a company's giving
- In the case of an owner-operated business the CEO can make a personal contribution to the foundation as well as leveraging the company's profits for the cause
- If endowed a foundation can provide a buffer for financial highs and lows. Companies can grow their endowments in profitable years and tap into them during leaner years
- Because of their reporting requirements foundations must be transparent. As a result employees and members of the community have an opportunity to have full exposure to the company's donations. This paves the way for engagement in a company's philanthropy program and can help counter any cynicism

And here are several challenges in developing a corporate foundation:

- A lot of bureaucracy is involved in setting up and maintaining a foundation. From filing incorporation papers to keeping records, time, staff and resources are required to keep the structure in place
- Foundations are limited in how their dollars can be used, which may conflict with the company's sense of autonomy in grant-making decisions
- Because a foundation legally is a distinct entity from the company itself it can create a barrier to employee engagement and participation

We recommend seeking legal guidance in understanding whether a foundation is best for your business.

Other resources:

- Association for Small Foundations
  www.smallfoundations.org
- Foundation Group
  www.501c3.org
- Hurwit and Associates
  www.hurwitassociates.com
- Philanthropic Foundations Canada
  www.pfc.ca

Managing Expectations

We recommend drafting a simple "letter of understanding" between you and your cause partner(s). In the letter list in general terms what you, the corporate partner, will provide (funds, in-kind product, volunteers, etc.) and what the charity will provide (communication, volunteer opportunities, etc.). If both parties acknowledge the commitments up front, challenges down the road can be avoided.

CONNECTION CHECKLIST

1. *Relevance/cause category*
2. *Focus: one or more?*
3. *Local or global reach?*
4. *Chemistry*
5. *Financial responsibility*
6. *Hands-on opportunities*
7. *Faith and religion*
8. *Sustainability*
9. *Exclusivity: other corporate partners*
10. *Administrative capabilities*
11. *Structure for giving*
12. *Managing expectations*

5

Step #3
Get Everyone Involved

What we do is only a drop in the ocean,
but if we didn't do it, the ocean would be one drop less.
— MOTHER THERESA

Imagine:

- A CEO, customer service rep and account manager side-by-side with sleeves rolled up swinging their hammers. They are in a city suburb, building a home for a family that doesn't have one
- Workers from a national corporation turning on a faucet at the end of the pipe that their co-workers helped villagers lay, that leads to the well that others in the company helped dig, providing clean drinking water for the first time to the people of a village in Guatemala
- Workers from a mid-sized pharmaceutical company playing chess with a group of inner-city youth to teach them the principle that their actions have consequences
- All of your employees jumping up at the company's annual meeting to applaud as a check is presented to the company's

charity partner, knowing that they all contributed to this moment — together

Connecting — Together

Strategic corporate philanthropy is not an exercise in writing checks. It's an exercise in connecting, contributing and making a difference. This chapter outlines in detail how everyone can participate and take ownership in the program, whether through something as simple as a payroll deduction or company paid volunteer time or skill exchanges and fundraising.

Spectrum Health Care and the Xalibe Project

For example, Spectrum Health Care has nurses and personal support workers providing care in homes across Metropolitan Toronto. In 2006 Spectrum launched a new, strategic approach to corporate giving. Not even a year into their initiative the benefits were being realized by a Guatemalan village and Spectrum's employees.

How did it happen?

Due to the nature of their work the Spectrum team rarely gets together. The company wanted to do something that would allow all of its employees to enjoy the same sense of community enjoyed by employees at most other firms. Xalibe is a village of about 35 families suffering extreme poverty as a result of the collapse of the coffee industry in their area. The village needed help setting priorities and developing new skills and resources.

Spectrum adopted this village through a partnership with Choice Humanitarian, helping villagers get on the road to better health. Xalibe's needs were so great that, even before announcing the initiative to employees, Spectrum management jumped in with support. They financed the completion of a water system for the village. Now, as a result of employee participation, a basic medical station will be built and supplied. And a few people in the village will be trained to improve the well-being of the entire community well past the life of the project. One nurse reflected the feelings of many Spectrum employees when she said, "This project gives us the chance to stretch out our hand to our fellow man and make the world a better place."

Enthusiasm has definitely been demonstrated: employees have pledged triple the anticipated financial support. This level of employee ownership is key to the success of Spectrum's philanthropy initiative. The Xalibe Project is now in their hands. While Spectrum's management will support their objectives, it is up to the employees — as a community — to carry it into the future.

The psychological rewards associated with giving can become part of your company's benefits program. The "values-added" proposition, as Mark Sarner, president of Manifest Communications, calls it, connects employees to each other, the company and the community.

Financial Contributions

There is no question that the number-one need of most non-profits is money. They require funding to operate and provide critical services to those in need. While we will suggest a number of non-monetary ways to contribute, it's important to remember that whatever else you may provide, cash is almost always needed, even if just to move your contribution to those in need.

As we've noted, corporate philanthropy historically has entailed the company writing a check, with the amount showing up as a line item — "charitable giving" — on the balance sheet. By providing employees with the opportunity to contribute you are not only giving them some ownership of the program but you are also giving them the opportunity to become inspired about making a difference.

Most of us *want* to give back but life gets in the way and we just don't get around to it. Evidence of this hard-wired human desire to give surfaces in times of crisis. After the horror of 9/11 in the US and the devastation caused by the tsunami in South Asia, as well as the many hurricanes that have buffeted the Caribbean and the US Southeast, people from every age bracket and socio-economic group stepped up to give. They did this through their own companies, online, at benefits — wherever and whenever they got the chance. Giving is in our nature. We just need the opportunity to give to be sincere, simple and right there in front of us. When employers integrate giving into their corporate culture, a collective soul of compassion emerges, leading to company pride. In this way the values vacuum is filled. The strong human need to give is fulfilled and employee loyalty and retention flourishes.

Payroll Deductions

The simplest and most convenient way for employees to contribute finances is through a payroll deduction. Like an RSP or 401k contribution deducted automatically from a paycheck, once it's set up, it accumulates impressively over time. We encourage our clients to set up "categories" for these contributions. Some clients come up with giving levels, like bronze, silver and gold. Employees may be given an opportunity to opt in or out of a giving program, or change their contribution amount, through a simple standard form available through human resources or the company intranet.

If this form is ready for the launch of the giving program (to be discussed in chapter 6), everyone can have a chance to enroll while emotion is strong. As for employees who join the firm post-launch, the opportunity to contribute should be offered to them as part of their orientation.

Some of your people may not be willing to commit to an ongoing payroll deduction right from the get-go, so we advise giving them the option of a one-time payroll deduction.

In-kind Product Contributions

Let's say your company produces a product that could make a difference to needy people. An effective contribution vehicle may be to give employees the opportunity to purchase the product at cost and contribute it as an in-kind donation. This can be done as a payroll deduction on its own, in conjunction with a straight cash contribution or as a separate, one-time or occasional giving opportunity. USANA Health Sciences, for example, gives all constituents the opportunity to provide a monthly contribution of their children's nutritional supplement, Usanimals, to children in the developing world.

Our clients who have taken this approach are astounded by the results. There's a reason the World Wildlife Fund encourages you to use your contribution to "adopt" a gorilla, or Global Partners for Development allows you to earmark your contribution to provide something real like a cow for a family or a sewing machine for a woman to start her own business. Whether making a donation of eyeglasses, toys, clothing or nutritional supplements, people like to contribute something tangible. When employees can donate a company's product or service they find renewed purpose in their daily work. They no longer see the product as simply a commodity but as a valuable item that makes a concrete difference.

It's important to set aside resources to fund the distribution of the product to ensure that it gets where it needs to go. That's why we encourage the monitoring of product-to-cash contribution levels to work toward getting the right balance.

Fundraisers

Designing short-term and long-term fundraising projects for employees on an ongoing basis creates excitement, enthusiasm and inspiration. Charitable projects can become great vehicles for team-building activities, even through creating healthy competition between departments and/or regional offices. There can be annual one-time fundraisers (walk-a-thons, golf tournaments, galas and the like) or short-term fundraisers (potluck lunches, denim days, raffles, etc.).

M·A·C Cosmetics' sole philanthropic focus is on AIDS. The company supports a wide range of organizations that provide basic needs, direct services, education, awareness and prevention programs to men, women and children affected by the disease. M·A·C employees organize themselves into teams to participate in various local fundraising events, such as runs. Lilia Garcia Levya, executive director of M·A·C's AIDS Fund, often receives an envelope of checks from an event organized by M·A·C employees that management wasn't even aware of: living proof that the power of the program has extended beyond the CEO and management team to truly become the heart and soul of the company.

Corporate Fund Matching

Matching employee contributions is a highly effective way for a company to demonstrate commitment to its employees and to the cause. This connects employees to management and creates a common purpose and a team environment, making for great workplaces.

Cause Days

Some companies designate a day each quarter or year as a cause day. It could mean that a percentage of the company's profits for the day goes to the cause.

On June 21, 2006 (the summer solstice), Robert Kent Photography held its first annual stock photo shoot fundraiser. A group of committed photographers, models, stylists, art directors, producers, assistants and volunteers donated their time and images to the Compassionate Eye Foundation stock contract with Getty Images. The foundation, which provides funding for children's education in the developing world, has committed to holding the event annually and growing it internationally. It expects to raise significant funds on this one day alone.

Specific Product Contribution

Your company could also design or choose an existing product to be the "cause product," designating an ongoing percentage of the sales of that product to the cause.

Pampered Chef's signature philanthropy program, Round-Up from the Heart, allows the company's consultants to promote and sell Seasons of the Heart Stoneware molds, with a portion of proceeds going to Second Harvest, the food-bank network.

One hundred percent of the selling price of M·A·C Cosmetics' lipstick VIVA GLAM goes to the M·A·C AIDS Fund. The funds are directed to local and geographic regions where the need for HIV-related care and services is greatest.

Custom Product Contribution

Your company may be able to custom-design a product for the cause, selling it to raise funds or giving it away to address a social need.

Roots is known around the world for its wide range of quality leather goods, clothing and accessories. When Hurricane Ivan devastated Jamaica, in 2004, and when later that year the tsunami hit South Asia, Roots, through the innovative efforts of the co-founders' daughters, immediately produced leather bracelets and sold them to raise money for relief. (For more on this, see chapter 8.)

Isagenix International is one of the world's fastest-growing manufacturers and distributors of nutritional products. The company is currently developing a product formulated to provide oral rehydration therapy to prevent and treat dehydration in the developing world. Customers will be able to purchase this product through Isagenix and have it distributed through the company's charity partner, Global Partners for Development.

Other Ways to Contribute

Skills Exchange

Enabling your employees to contribute their skills in support of your cause or non-profit is one of the most valuable resources you may ever give. Perhaps your marketing department can help with a campaign for the cause, or your legal people can draft an agreement or register a legal document, or your IT specialist can help them set up a new system. Some companies will lend a specialist to their charity for an extended period to help them complete a project. And there may be someone in the target charity or a particular company with a specific skill that can help you out — a true exchange!

Jeff Flug, CEO of Millennium Promise, tells Orenda that receiving expertise from companies has been invaluable. One of their corporate partners is in the process of designing a program that will second (loan) company employees bearing specific expertise for a three- to six-month period. This will allow Millennium Promise to leverage its own capabilities while maintaining a very low overhead.

One of Orenda's banking clients has partnered with a local non-profit that runs a number of homeless shelters. This company not only adopts families to support at Christmas each year but also sends employees in from time to time to teach basic family budgeting skills, helping these folks get back on their feet. In a letter sent after his first visit to the shelter, one employee said, "It was the most inspiring thing I have ever experienced."

Volunteer Time

By giving your employees paid time to volunteer for your cause you are authentically demonstrating your company's commitment to making a difference. This can be the single most effective way to increase the level of inspiration in your workplace. The buzz will start and the good karma will begin to flow as your people return to work with powerful stories from the field. Most companies specify a certain number of volunteer hours that employees are able to contribute. They may be spread over a year or taken all at once. Our advice is to make it paid time.

At Luxottica Retail involvement with Gift of Sight begins at the store level where employees are empowered to help the needy in their communities. Those who want to do more can step up to serve as a Gift of Sight Store Captain, then regional Gift of Sight Captain and/or coordinator of a regional Vision Van mission. Finally, they can apply for a coveted spot on an international or North American mission. Team members are selected based on involvement in and leadership of local activities. The volunteer hierarchy and goal of being selected for a two-week, all-expenses-paid experience of a lifetime (on payroll!) helps fuel program leadership. Luxottica employees deliver Gift of Sight programs on company and on personal time. The company supports Gift of Sight participation on work time because of its proven ability to develop employee pride, recruit and retain top talent, offer powerful team-building opportunities and provide meaningful leadership training and diversity experiences.

Business Community Support

Letting your suppliers and customers know about your program gives you the opportunity to extend your philanthropic reach outside the walls of the company.

When Spectrum Health Care announced it was adopting the village of Xalibe in Guatemala one of their suppliers stepped up with wheelchairs and blood-pressure kits, valuable contributions to health care in the village. When USANA had a raffle to raise money for the Children's Hunger Fund™ various suppliers provided valuable raffle prizes. By effectively communicating your program (see the following chapter) you will find that many members of the community will step up to contribute.

Your giving program doesn't need to begin with all of the above initiatives in place. This is simply a list of possibilities and suggestions to help get you going. In time you may end up integrating many or all of these methods.

Snapshots of Inspirational Involvement

Timberland/City Year

A shared vision of community has led Timberland and City Year to create fun and engaging projects in the spirit of strengthening communities. For example, City Year has organized a number of projects for Timberland employees, including its annual global Serv-a-Palooza and Earth Day projects. These are 6,000-person events in which the entire company gives the community two days of volunteer service.

Value statements that are key to both organizations' philosophies, such as Give Racism a Boot and Hike the Path to Justice, were placed on backpacks and T-shirts and marketed through Timberland's retail outlets, with the profits going to City Year.

As a regular part of their collaboration the two organizations engage in executive exchanges in which the skills of one organization are leveraged to benefit the other. This commitment to reciprocity is what makes the relationship so powerful. It is in fact the true spirit of community at work.

Fortune magazine has included Timberland in its 100 Best Companies to Work For list over the past many years, citing the company's service program as a factor in its selection.

The Home Depot and KaBOOM!

The Home Depot, the world's largest home-improvement specialty retailer, has partnered with KaBOOM!, a non-profit dedicated to improving communities by building and renovating playgrounds and skateparks in "children-rich and playground-poor" markets. Since the mid-1990s The Home Depot has contributed millions of dollars, high-quality building materials and the volunteer efforts of tens of thousands of Team Depot Associates, who join residents of the community to build safe places for kids to play.

Having already funded approximately 400 KaBOOM! Playgrounds, The Home Depot and KaBOOM! announced, in the summer of 2005, "1000 playspaces in 1000 days," an initiative that will take three years, $25 million and over a million volunteer hours. It is expected to benefit 1.5 million parents and children.

The Giving Statement

Strategies for designing a company Giving Statement have been discussed throughout the preceding chapters. By walking through these questions you should now know:

- Why you're giving (purpose)
- Whom you're giving to (cause)
- Where you're giving (local or global)
- How and when you're giving (contribution program)

A simple statement incorporating the decisions you have made will work as a reference for decision making about your initiative. Here's the formula:

> In order to (*why — purpose*), we (*company*) support (*cause, locally or globally*) through a program that includes (*how, when*).

Calendar and Budget

Like any other corporate initiative an annual Contribution Activity Plan, designed in advance, will help integrate your program into your business plan. Look at your year-at-a-glance document and identify opportunities in connection with other corporate initiatives, holidays and celebrations. This planning will also allow you to prepare a corresponding budget.

INVOLVEMENT CHECKLIST
Financial contributions:
- *Payroll deductions*
- *In-kind product contributions*
- *Fundraisers*
- *Corporate fund matching*
- *Cause day*
- *Specific product contributions*
- *Custom product contributions*

Other ways to contribute
- *Skills exchange*
- *Volunteer time*
- *Business community support*

The Giving Statement
Calendar and Budget

---

(6)

Step #4
Start Spreading the News

Always do right — this will
gratify some and astonish the rest.
— MARK TWAIN

As with all company initiatives, launching the initiative takes a thrust of energy, while keeping it soaring requires a commitment to consistent, creative communication. The latter is what this chapter is about. It gives you a go-to communications checklist, including tips on everything from corporate events to Web, e-mail, newsletter and marketing efforts to decking the halls of the office with visuals to integrating the program into the company's new employee orientation.

Branding Your Giving Initiative

Creating a brand for your giving program will help you develop an identity for it within your corporate brand. Branding gives it a name that will become recognized as your giving program. People often reduce "brand" in this context to a logo. But in branding, a logo is part of a much larger, deliberate effort to articulate the brand idea in a way that elicits a particular response.

So before you select a nifty typeface for your logo take a step back and think of your brand in this broader context. Advertising professionals go through an extensive creative process when they are defining a commercial brand concept. You can shorthand this process, however, by asking these simple questions:

1. What's the one most important thing we want this brand to convey about our philanthropy initiative?
2. What three adjectives would we use to describe our unique approach to giving?
3. Who is our target audience and what do they care about? What will motivate them rationally, emotionally?

Oprah's Angel Network

A good example of this kind of branding is Oprah's Angel Network, a public charity formed in 1998 to inspire people around the world to make a difference. Oprah's network supports charitable projects and provides grants to non-profit organizations around the globe that share in this vision. Given her brand focus on inspiring others it's no wonder that she has focused her network's communications efforts on stories. On her show and Website she gives awards to inspiring individuals, encouraging and motivating others to create social change in their own way. Yes, Oprah's Angel Network has a name and a logo. More importantly, however, it has an identity that fits her identity and that people can relate to.

The Gift of Sight

In 1988 LensCrafters created Give the Gift of Sight, a family of charitable vision care programs that provide free eye care and glasses to those in need in their communities and in developing countries around the world. The name "Gift of Sight" perfectly conveys LensCrafters' belief that good eyesight is a basic human right, not a luxury. In addition the Gift of Sight's dedicated Website provides graphic examples of how glasses and eye exams are transforming lives.

ninemillion.org

Microsoft and Nike have joined forces with the United Nations High Commissioner to create ninemillion.org, an organization that "owns" the plight of the world's nine million child refugees. By putting a number on their cause the organization makes the task of helping these children seem realistic and doable. The name puts a finite number to the social challenge. It is a fact-based campaign that makes a straightforward case for giving.

The Xalibe Project

As mentioned earlier in this book Spectrum Health Care is helping Xalibe, a Guatemalan village of about 35 families who are suffering from the collapse of the coffee industry. Spectrum chose a specific village to support because it wanted its contributions to be meaningful both to recipients and contributors. Calling the program the Xalibe Project reminds people that all of their hard work and energy is being focused on a specific place with very dire needs. Spectrum calls it a "project" to make it clear that the initiative has a beginning and an end and that the effort will eventually be self-sustaining.

Launch Events

Depending on the size of your organization and the nature of your business you may or may not hold regular corporate events. Sales meetings, quarterly employee meetings, regional office meetings, annual company conferences — no matter what your meeting structure and schedule may be, your program will be most effective if it is launched when your people are together. You can make the launch an individual item on a meeting agenda or make it the only item on the agenda of a specially called meeting.

Launch time is the best time to inspire your workplace. This is your chance to send the message of how important the program is and how important employee involvement is — to send the message that their support and involvement are not something you merely hope for but something you are going to encourage, through giving company time and resources to employees and constituents who want to participate.

This approach will introduce them to, or further their awareness of, your company's corporate soul. It will give them the sense that they are in the right place, working for the right company.

Make the launch special. Make it a surprise. Make it visual, emotional and personal.

The corporate leader should be the one to announce a new program, from center stage or center field, inviting employees to join management in supporting the cause. Have written material ready for them: a description of the cause, expected outcomes, how people can get involved, contribution forms and sign-up sheets. Invite a representative from the cause to be there to meet employees and answer questions.

As you launch the program, launch the contribution plan, too. Help employees see how they can take ownership of the program and how they can contribute.

Emily Franson, director of Community Outreach for Choice Humanitarian, had this to say in an interview with Orenda:

A launch of the program is crucial. We learned this with Spectrum Health Care. Of all the partnerships to that point, Spectrum was the most successful because of the powerful, emotional launch. There is power and momentum when people are together, outside of work, celebrating something good. That momentum can then translate to the rest of the company.

Ongoing Events

Anytime you bring your people together is an opportunity to affirm the company's commitment to the cause. Make it part of the agenda. Through updates, visuals, stories and speakers you can keep it front and center as a corporate initiative. You can confirm for employees that the cause is extending the company's mission beyond the balance sheet by letting them hear from representatives of the charity or the group receiving the benefits. This will breathe life into the program for them. At each USANA event we had Dave Phillips, president of Children's Hunger Fund™, give us an update. It was particularly inspiring to also have a director of one of the orphanages present, not only to thank USANA employees for their contributions but also to speak to the difference that the nutritional product contributions were making to the health of children.

Website

As part of the launch of the program post on your Website a description of the program and opportunities for contribution. You may want to provide a link to your charity partner's Website. Appoint someone from your giving team to update the site regularly as the project progresses.

In writing this book we have collected URLs of Websites containing creative and innovative examples of how companies have integrated giving programs into their corporate culture. We list many of them in the sources section at the end of this book. There are thousands of great stories out there. We suggest you visit the sites of some of the businesses you support, as well.

Newsletters/e-zines/e-mails/blogs

Use any communication medium in your company's arsenal to let everyone in your company — and anyone else who subscribes to any of these communications — know what you're doing. Always provide the link to the page on your Website that describes your program and how to contribute to it.

Your giving program deserves some real estate in your newsletter. Assign someone on your steering committee to gather information for each issue or posting. It needs to include an update on the project and employee activities. Your contact at the non-profit is a great resource for concrete information. Be sure to give this person your company publication/posting dates and deadlines, so they can prepare their submissions well in advance.

Visuals

A picture is worth a thousand words.

Once your program is under way leave a trail of evidence around your workplace — for example, photographs from the launch and of any hands-on volunteer activities. These photos will spread the news in a way that words can never do. Depending on what the activities are, plan to have a video camera available to document them. Doing this will capture great material for your Website or to show at subsequent events.

Every time Dr. Wentz or any USANA employees traveled to one of the company's project sites we made sure a video camera was there to document it. We then edited the video, added some voiceover or moving music and played it at every company event. This turned out to be the most compelling way to communicate the commitment of the CEO to the cause and to show employees the effect of their contributions. Watching the children receive their vitamins brought home to employees how effective their giving truly was. Their commitment grew each successive year, which served to integrate the program ever more securely into the culture of the company. As the visuals inspired the corporate soul the business grew dramatically.

New Employee Orientation

No matter how new employees are introduced to the policies, procedures and purpose of your company, make sure you include in the process an introduction to your philanthropy program. Let them know how they can contribute. Inform them of any current fundraising initiatives or programs.

Recognition

Babies cry for it — grown men and women die for it.

Company recognition programs are an integral part of corporate soul and inspiration. When done authentically and with meaning they can have a profoundly positive impact.

We're not suggesting you recognize people for the *level* of their contribution. Instead create something related to the giving program that they can earn. You could even integrate this into your other internal work-related recognition programs.

For example, one of our clients is launching a project that involves giving to a program in Africa. This company has made it possible for employees to earn a trip to Africa to participate more directly in the project. While this may not appeal to everyone it certainly will appeal to some — in fact many will go to great lengths to earn it. This specific incentive is becoming part of a company-wide incentive program related to the cause, with different departments creating different work-related performance criteria for earning the trip.

Another example is Spectrum Health Care. Through its Spirit of

Spectrum Award employees can nominate fellow employees to be recognized for their community citizenship in the workplace. The winners, along with the company COO, spend a week at Xalibe, the village that Spectrum adopted in Guatemala.

Some of our clients allow employees to earn additional volunteer days.

Pampered Chef allocates points in its incentive program for each volunteer day an employee works for Second Harvest, the food-bank network.

Marketing

Whether or not to include your philanthropy program in your marketing initiatives is an individual company decision. There are two schools of thought. One is that companies exploit their giving program by promoting it, thus missing the whole point of giving. The other is that more and more consumers want to know which companies are giving back and how they're doing it — they want to support socially responsible businesses, especially ones that are also creating inspiring places to work.

Talk to the marketing agencies and they'll side with the second school. Pamela Divinsky is a VP at Ethos, a new division of the advertising agency JWT in Toronto that was designed to meet the boom in social marketing. She is quoted in *Strategy* magazine as saying: "People have said to corporations that the footprint that you make on the world is bigger than just your office tower or your manufacturing plant." She adds that "consumers are looking for sources of meaning and trust — something a bit deeper."

Tony Piggot, the president/CEO of JWT Canada, says in the same article that marketing your cause is "taking a meaningful stance on something, doing something about it and then communicating it. People can separate tokenism from something real."

This is no small trend. The week of festivities at the Cannes Lions in June 2006 included an exhibit by ACT Responsible (Advertising Community Together) called Taking Care of Our Future, which showcased about 400 advertising campaigns with a focus on social and environmental issues.

Here are some ways, as detailed by Philip Kotler and Nancy Lee in *Corporate Social Responsibility*, to communicate your giving to your customers and the community:

- Marketing materials: catalogues, brochures, product labels, point-of-sale visuals
- Media advertising: print, television, radio, Web
- Sponsorships: A company can visibly support a charitable event or activity. For example, a major Canadian bank, the Canadian Imperial Bank of Commerce, has title sponsorship of the Canadian Breast Cancer Foundation's (CBCF) Run for the Cure. In exchange for its name in the event's title (CIBC Run for the Cure) the bank provides financial support and an enormous team of volunteers. CIBC's name and logo are highly visible on all marketing materials (brochures, posters, etc.), and their affiliation with the event is promoted in every one of its branch locations across Canada. In 2005 Imagine Canada honored CIBC for its contribution to CBCF by granting it the prestigious Business and Community Partnership Award
- Corporate social marketing: Rather than directly promoting an affiliation with a cause, social marketing enables a company to author a social message or support a public education campaign. This kind of marketing allows the company to stand for something without directly promoting its good works. For example, Ericsson Communications launched its Ericsson Response program with an advertisement that called on other companies to come forward to help create a better

solution to natural disasters. Ericsson's logo was at the bottom of the advertisement, but the message focused on how the world still doesn't have an adequate way to respond to people in crisis situations

Consumers Will Reward Companies That Meet Their Expectations

In 2004 the Boston-based strategic marketing firm Cone released its Cone Corporate Citizenship Report. The CEO of the firm, Carole Cone, said in a press release of December 8, 2004: "This study, in a series of research spanning over a decade, shows that in today's climate, more than ever before, companies must get involved with social issues in order to protect and enhance their reputations."

The study, the nation's longest study of American attitudes toward corporate support of social issues, shows that "eight in 10 Americans say that corporate support of causes wins their trust in that company, a 21% increase since 1997." It emphasizes that companies must talk more about their cause-related efforts.

> Some companies have recognized the positive impact of supporting social issues, and have aggressively communicated their efforts over the past few years. At the same time, many other companies have traditionally been reluctant about such communications, seeing them as boastful. An overwhelming majority of Americans (86%) want companies to talk about their efforts, but only four in 10 say companies are doing that well.

The study also points out that young Americans are more likely to support good corporate citizens.

> As young Americans demonstrated unparalleled participation in the 2004 presidential election, seeking a leader who shared

their values, they also continued to voice high expectations of companies to be solid corporate citizens. Cone's research shows that Americans 18-25 years old are significantly more likely to consider a company's citizenship practices when making purchasing, employment and investment decisions.

"Today's young adults have learned to become savvy consumers and have recognized the importance of a company standing for something that they believe in," says Cone. "Our research shows that cause-related activities will influence not only their buying habits, but also gain their loyalty and trust. Aligning with a cause is a significant strategy for companies to attract consumers and a future workforce at an early age and gain a long-term, sustainable competitive advantage."

For Consumers or Employees?

Celebrating your philanthropy program in your marketing material can do more for your employees than your customers.

Deloitte and Touche took out a full-page ad in the *Globe and Mail*, a national paper in Canada, to thank employees for participating in its annual volunteer day. According to Mark Sarner of Manifest Communications, "The ad probably meant little to clients — but it was huge for employees. It showed the employees that this was important to the company and strengthened that bond of connection and engagement. There's no comparison between the impact of a thank you on the bulletin board, and a thank you on a full page of your newspaper."

Calendar and Budget

Each communication effort will have a related expense — some more than others. First, decide which communication vehicles are best suited to your business model and culture. Second, connect your communication plan to your contribution activity plan.

Finally, integrate these two plans into your communication calendar, with corresponding budget requirements.

COMMUNICATION CHECKLIST

- *Branding your giving program*
- *Launch event*
- *Ongoing events*
- *Website*
- *Newsletters/e-zines/e-mails/blogs*
- *Visuals*
- *New employee orientation*
- *Recognition*
- *Marketing*

Calendar and budget

Step #5
Measure and Grow

If you find it in your heart to care
for someone else, you will have succeeded.
— MAYA ANGELOU

In the karmic context how do you know whether your philanthropy program is successful — whether what's going around to help those in need is coming around to strengthen your corporate culture?

When the stakes are low, measuring success doesn't really matter. For example, if a canvasser from a charity comes to your door and solicits a $40 check from you, you're unlikely to expect anything in return (besides a tax receipt and a thank you). The same is true of check-writing philanthropy. The exchange is fairly simple and the expectations fairly low. The company writing the check doesn't expect a significant return on investment.

When the stakes are high, however, measurement matters. A savvy charity will do its best to enhance its relationship with the company, hoping to increase the donation and deepen the nature of the relationship. And savvy companies, meanwhile, will raise their expectations as their giving becomes more significant. They will want to measure the return on their charitable giving, just as they do with any of their substantial and strategic long-term business commitments.

It's no surprise, then, that our clients often ask these two related questions:

- "How do we know that our corporate contribution is making a difference in the lives of people it's intended to help?"
- "How can I tell if my employees, stakeholders and customers are engaged in our company's corporate philanthropy program?"

Measuring Social Impact

Many attempts have been made to establish criteria for measuring a charity's effectiveness in doing its job. A few key resources, including Charity Navigator, Guidestar and a dedicated issue of *Worth Magazine*, rank non-profits' performance in the US. Rankings of Canada's non-profits may be found at Imagine Canada. However, while these organizations are good at providing snapshots of charitable organizations' operations, they are not able to track the impact of particular contributions.

Sometimes the task of measuring social change is easy. Because Spectrum Health Care's contributions were focused on providing a water line and free-standing health-post to the Guatemalan village of Xalibe, measurement was relatively straightforward. Once it was done it was done. However, Spectrum also wanted to know the health outcomes of its contribution. Would the conditions that were the result of contaminated water diminish over time? Would the health post continue to help the village meet its health needs? On the surface it seems that measurement of these matters would also be straightforward. But as any researcher will tell you, even easy-to-track numbers can be thrown off by such variables as a particularly rainy season or the influx of a new virus into the village.

As Marc Benioff and Karen Southwick write in their book *Compassionate Capitalism*:

> With philanthropy, it's difficult to produce precise periodic measurements, and even if you do, they can be meaningless. A homeless shelter, no doubt, can tell you how many meals it serves each day to how many people. But if it's serving fewer meals, does that mean the number of homeless is decreasing or the food is lousy?

It's essential that companies work closely with their charitable partners to establish objectives and measures that *can* be used to benchmark success. This step can be part of the agreement so that it is clear to everyone how success will be measured.

Dave Phillips, president of Children's Hunger Fund™, is clear on the results of USANA's contribution. In an interview he said:

> The impact on children has been substantial. Currently, about 5,000 children in selected countries receive daily nutritional supplements, many of whom came into our program malnourished or HIV infected. The health benefits have been dramatic — measurable weight gain, improved appetite, 75% reduction in illness, marked improvement developmentally, etc. Some of the funding has been used to provide food distribution to needy families, providing villages with greater access to nutritional food and other resources such as shoes, clothing, hygiene items, etc. The partnership has also allowed us to begin to provide nutrition/hygiene education to some of the poorest areas around the world.
>
> Other measurable benefits have been in some of the refugee camps in Africa, where USANA funds have been used to provide

emergency food shipments. One such camp we support was home to 33,000 children two years ago. As a result of USANA's help, malnutrition has been reduced by more than 95% since then. Resettlement programs that we support have also reduced the population in the camps by more than 70% as families leave and are provided with the means to build homes and grow their own crops to sustain themselves.

Through the medical centers in Uganda and Cambodia that Dr. Wentz has personally funded we have been able to provide thousands of village families and orphan children in our programs with direct access to emergency health care, diagnostic treatment, regular health exams and preventative education.

Tangibly speaking, thousands of young lives have been spared from starvation and malnutrition; others have been given a reprieve from seizures due to malaria and other intestinal illnesses.

Reporting specific quantitative results and outcomes will bring a philanthropy program to life for everyone contributing to it.

Discussions should be held within your company and between your company and the charity to determine what is reasonable to expect in one year, five years, 10 years and out. Metrics should then be created to measure the results, as well as to hold the non-profit accountable for reporting back. It is also important to clarify who will bear the costs and responsibility of reporting progress. If it is part of the non-profit's regular practice to track progress, they can provide information on a quarterly, semi-annual or annual basis. In the case of a more complex project or where the non-profit does not have the capability to report, the company will bear the responsibility of developing a sound methodology for charting impact over time.

No matter who takes the lead it is essential that corporations take the long view of social change. Unlike the jump in sales that

Apple saw when it introduced the iPod, social change takes time. How long will it take to eliminate poverty and hunger on the planet? How long will it take to make a significant dent in the AIDS epidemic? Measuring progress on these issues is very different from tracking quarterly profits.

There are, however, some ways to break these issues down, measuring social impact incrementally. Companies can note such things as:

- An increase in use of a charity's products or services (more shelter beds, greater access to treatment, more low-income homes built)
- A decrease in a negative behavior or condition (fewer computers to landfills, reduction in the incidence of a disease, a decrease in drinking and driving)
- The presence of a new initiative (new health post created, new public awareness campaign launched)
- The ratio of dollars spent in administration (fundraising, marketing, etc.) to dollars spent in the field providing a direct service to those in need

Measuring the Impact on Business

Throughout this book we have emphasized the transformational power of corporate philanthropy: its ability to change corporate culture, inspire employees, increase employee retention and loyalty and create customer loyalty. These are significant claims and they are supported by a plethora of research studies undertaken worldwide.

It is essential for you to identify the business objectives under-lying a strategic corporate philanthropy program. Do you want the program to help you attract the best talent? Is employee loyalty an issue in your competitive marketplace? The reason we call it *strategic* corporate philanthropy is that a program can be designed to address specific problems or issues.

Following are four main ways to measure the business impact of corporate philanthropy programs. Depending on the scope of measurement you're looking for you could be well advised to hire a research firm to gather the information. You may be tempted to develop a survey or conduct a focus group on your own, but to get accurate answers, questions have to be asked the right way, and that does require expertise. For suggestions of research firms that specialize in these measurements contact info@orenda connections.com.

Quantitative Research

Most people who work in companies today are regularly asked to complete surveys. The surveys, whether online or paper-based, ask questions that get at a range of experiences, beliefs and attitudes. Quantitative research is an effective tool to create a baseline snapshot of employee beliefs and attitudes, against which success can be tracked over time.

In the case of corporate philanthropy, surveys can ask the obvious questions, such as: Are you aware of which charities your company supports? Have you participated in an event or activity associated with a charitable cause? It is more challenging to formulate questions that measure the effects of philanthropy on the softer issues of employee satisfaction, loyalty, motivation and connectedness to the company's mission, but skillful researchers can craft questions to create a profile of a company's corporate culture.

Qualitative Research

Most people picture focus groups as involving high-powered executives scrutinizing participants trapped in a sterile room through a one-way mirror. But focus groups have grown up. The settings are a lot more innovative and attractive — and sometimes the groups don't get together at all but participate instead from the comfort of their homes or offices through an online thread.

The advantage of qualitative research is that it can get at information in a much more detailed and textured way. You walk away not with mere data but with quotes and analysis. Expert researchers know how to dig deeper than surveys can go, garnering important insights about core issues.

That said, CEOs and senior leaders often do need hard facts to satisfy shareholders and stakeholders. What to do?

Combined Approach

The best solution is a combination of qualitative and quantitative research. Surveys provide hard data that can make it easy to track success in a tangible way. Focus groups, meanwhile, can get at softer, more complex issues to suss out the real story of what's happening in an organization. Quantitative research can report the percentage of a company that feels loyal or not. Qualitative research can take up the baton and determine the factors causing workers to stay or leave, such as the competitiveness of the marketplace, the appropriateness of pay and how challenging the work is.

An Alternate Approach: Taking the Pulse

Without exception the CEOs who have pioneered the strongest and most notable corporate philanthropy programs say that the driving force behind their programs is the sense that it was "the right thing to do" as well as a belief that it's "good for business." Ask them how they know and they'll tell you they know it in their gut and because they can feel renewed energy in their employees as they walk the company's halls.

Making a commitment to corporate philanthropy takes a

combination of head and heart. The head part can be measured through the many tools we've listed above and the data provided throughout this book. The heart part is intangible, having to do with the soul of the company and the character of its decision makers.

Because it's considered a "softer" business strategy, philanthropy is sometimes the target of overzealous quantitative attempts to prove its impact. Our advice is to measure the impact of your philanthropy program through formal means if that is the culture of your organization. But feedback to the program and walking the floor will often provide you with far more insight than the graphs and charts of the research firms.

Here are some simple ways to get a read on the business success of your philanthropy program:

- Employee contributions over time
- Employee volunteer participation
- Employee event participation
- Employee in-kind contributions
- Customer participation
- Shareholder feedback
- Awards, rankings of Best Places to Work and corporate citizenship leadership
- Media relations hits

If your program is successful the buzz will speak for itself. In fact you won't be able to miss it. You'll feel the good karma.

Growing the Distance

The S Curve

To everything there is a season. Ideas that come to life don't stay alive forever. Like everything else, with time the inspirational effects of your philanthropy program will reach maturity. We're not suggesting that the cause or partner be changed when that happens. We are suggesting that you shake the program up from time to time to provide new opportunities for involvement, participation and outcome.

Give the program time to take root. The life of your program will follow the same S curve of all good new programs (see chart below). The first year will generally be the formulation period as your team designs and begins the rollout of your program. Year two will be a year of concentration, when roots begin to take hold and the brand takes on an identity. By year three the program will move toward reaching critical mass, taking on a life of its own and gaining momentum. Go with this momentum until you notice a leveling out of energy and enthusiasm. Regroup and refresh the program with new activities and opportunities.

Surviving the Storm

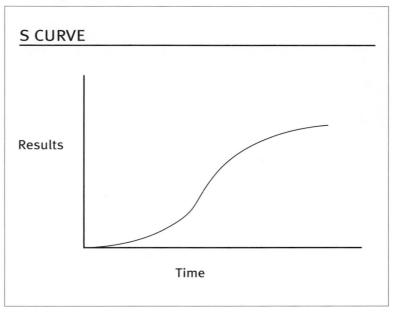

S CURVE

Results

Time

Nothing stays the same. Business is always changing. Leaders can come and go. Mergers and acquisitions can render a business unrecognizable. Economic ups and downs can open or close the checkbook in a heartbeat. Market conditions, natural disasters, technological advances — all can all have a dramatic impact on every initiative of your business. How will your philanthropy program survive?

The answer is found in the corporate soul. If times are challenging for your business, chances are they are for others, too. All the karmic wisdom we've discussed in this book speaks to the need to find a way to keep corporate values alive, even during the tough times — especially during the tough times. Change creates insecurity and instability and can have a dramatic impact on employee morale. However, if values are the touchstone for the company, employees will take comfort in that certainty and mobilize to survive the storm.

The program may change. Perhaps there will be more personal volunteer time than cash contributions. Maybe you'll have a square dance instead of a gala. Be prepared. Design a list of activities in advance as a fallback plan for challenging times. The important thing is to not only continue to support your program during hard times, but to actually hold it up as a lighthouse to guide the company's soul through the storm.

MEASUREMENT CHECKLIST

Measuring the impact on business:

1. *Quantitative — surveys*
2. *Qualitative — focus groups*
3. *Combined approach*
4. *Checking the pulse*
   - *Employee contributions over time*
   - *Employee volunteer participation*
   - *Employee event participation*
   - *Employee in-kind contributions*
   - *Customer participation*
   - *Stakeholder feedback*
   - *Awards, rankings of Best Places to Work and corporate citizenship leadership*
   - *Media hits*
5. *Growing the Distance*
   - The S curve: regroup and refresh
   - Surviving the storm: design a fallback plan

PART 3

Trends in Giving Together

(8)

Can't Buy Me Love
The Evolution of the Workforce

*It is one of the most beautiful compensations of life,
that no man can sincerely try to help another
without helping himself.*
— RALPH WALDO EMERSON

I ran across this insightful comment about our times quoted in the *Seattle Post-Intelligencer*: "As boomers retire, employers find they're fishing for talent in a puddle instead of a pool."

The Economist reports that when the Corporate Executive Board, a provider of business research and executive education based in Washington, D.C., conducted an international poll of senior human-resources managers recently, three-quarters of them said that "attracting and retaining" talent was their number-one priority.

And Steve Maich writes in *Maclean's* magazine:

> There was a time when all it took to be considered a good employer was to provide jobs for a lot of people. Offer competitive wages, basic benefits, make money and keep growing — that's all there was to it. Not anymore. With

101

Canada in the midst of its biggest job boom in more than a generation, millions of workers find themselves able to pick and choose between career paths. Today's job hunter isn't just looking for a steady paycheque, but a constant challenge, and *a career that's going to enrich life away from the office*. And just because you're able to attract talented people, it's no guarantee you'll be able to hold onto them.

Corporate Metamorphosis

Recent cases of corporate greed and corruption have had a profound and evolutionary impact on the corporation. Corporate leadership is now under a microscope and could in fact be at the "creative edge of human evolution," according to Elisabet Sahtouris, evolutionary biologist, futurist, author, consultant and fellow of the World Business Academy. Her company, Lifeweb — Living System Design, shows the relevance of biological systems to organizational design in business. "Corporate leadership can learn from biological evolution how to harmonize corporate with personal and community goals," she says on her Website.

The transformation of the caterpillar to a butterfly could be a great metaphor for our current corporate situation.

Before beginning to weave the chrysalis that will produce the butterfly the caterpillar goes through an extraordinary period of gluttony and over-consumption, during which it outgrows its own skin a number of times. Finally, guided by its DNA, a group of cells emerge in the caterpillar saying, "Enough is enough." They overpower the greedy cells and cause the caterpillar to shed its final skin to create the "nutritive soup" inside the chrysalis from which the beauty of the butterfly will emerge.

Is this the point we've reached in our corporate evolution? Like a caterpillar becoming a butterfly are we morphing from greed to giving, from profit to purpose, from destroying to restoring?

All the research points to an affirmative answer.

As the next generation of employees heads confidently and purposefully into the workforce, the landscape has changed dramatically from where it was for their parents. A profound shift has occurred in their vision and expectations. What work and career mean to them is not the same as it was a generation ago. They are weaving "making a living" and "designing a life" together to create a lifestyle tapestry that generations before them were not aware of or able to create for themselves.

As *Business Week* announced in August 2005, "A new generation of employees is demanding attention to stakeholders and seeking more from their jobs than just 9-to-5 work hours and a steady paycheck."

The 2006 Cone Millennial Cause Study, the first in-depth study of its kind, shows that 61% of Millennials, those born between 1979 and 2001, feel personally responsible for making a difference in the world. This civic-minded generation, 78 million strong, not only believes it is their personal responsibility to make the world a better place, but also believe (78% of them) that companies have a responsibility to join them in this effort. Millennials say they are prepared to reward or punish a company based on its commitment to social causes.

What is behind this enormous shift from the boomers and their inward focus (they are known as the "me generation") to younger workers and their increasing focus on establishing higher meaning and purpose in their work lives?

The first important factor is the dissatisfaction of the boomers, whose troubles with work were observed by their children — today's workforce. In a *Fast Company* article Harriet Rubin states that "baby boomers were raised on ambition and are a generation that is never happy with what it has. When everything comes too easily, all you want is more. Ambition is the longest unrequited love affair of boomers' lives."

The children of boomers watched their ambitious parents be downsized after years of loyalty. And they have seen corporate corruption reach new heights and seen mergers and acquisitions that have created an eerie idea of what exactly "a company" is. The younger generation no longer believes they can trust "their company" to look out for their best interests. They believe they have to take care of themselves and make choices that best meet their own needs. This is the generation not of Roger Moore but of Michael Moore. They are challenging the system and its failures.

At the same time, with longer work hours and the dual-worker family, work has become a larger and more significant part of life than ever before. So much so that authors John Izzo and Pam Withers, in their book *Values Shift*, say the reaction to this phenomenon is, "Now that work is life, it had better be a good one." The needs once met by community, religion and civil society must all be satisfied by the workplace. It's a tall order, but companies that are ahead of the curve will hold the advantage in attracting and retaining the best of the next generation of workers.

Employers need to pay attention. As each year of graduating students enters the work force their expectation that they will be allowed — and even encouraged — to combine purpose and passion in the work they do is becoming more and more apparent.

"It's a more educated, affluent work force," Mark Sussman of the New York employment-law firm Jackson, Lewis, Schnitzler & Krupman is quoted as saying in *Values Shift*. "They don't feel that a job is an asset that they're lucky to have. They have greater expectations."

This generation may have grown up with designer jeans and sneakers, video games and cellphones. Yet their yearning to earn in order to get the "stuff" that demonstrates success is not nearly as significant a driving force in their career and job decisions as for previous generations. Many of them have had so much and take so much for granted, it's as if their dreams, goals and values have moved at warp speed, causing them in their teens and 20s to ask unusually thoughtful questions about their purpose in life.

Meanwhile, they are being met in the middle by boomers who are leaving the workforce early in order to give prime years of their lives to good works at home and abroad.

Instead of getting whiplash as they watch these two generations come and go, savvy companies will capture, and benefit from, the philanthropic desire the generations are expressing.

Enter the Youth

Ryan Hreljac

In January 1998 six-year-old Ryan Hreljac of Kemptville, Ontario, listened intently as his first-grade teacher talked about the plight of people in Africa who had to walk many miles every day just to fetch water, the most basic element for human survival. Ryan was shocked and decided he needed to build a well for a village in Africa. He ran home from school and begged his parents for $70 — the amount he thought was needed. They eventually agreed to let him do extra chores to earn the money.

Four months later when Ryan delivered the money to a charity that builds wells in Africa, he learned that $70 was enough for only a hand pump, and that a well would actually cost $2,000. Undeterred, he said, "I'll just have to do more chores."

Ryan's tenacity touched the hearts of many adults, gave hope and life to many others and sparked an unrelenting string of media interviews and speaking engagements. He did raise the money for a well, then went on to raise funds for a drilling rig and many more wells. In the process he developed a vision: a world where everyone has clean water. His organization, the Ryan's Well Foundation, has helped raise over $1.5 million and has supported more than 245 water sources (wells, protected springs, water-harvesting tanks) in 11 developing countries, eight of which are in Africa.

Deeva Green

When Hurricane Ivan left a path of destruction throughout the Caribbean in September 2004, Deeva Green of Toronto, then just 15, decided to make a difference. Every year Deeva and her family spent their winter vacation in Jamaica, and she ached to help the people there, who had become like family to her. With the support of a family business she and her girlfriend, Alex Budman, designed bracelets in the colors of the Jamaican, Grenadian and Haitian flags and stood at the corner of Bloor and Bedford Streets in their city, selling them for $5 each. Their goal was to raise $2,000. To their amazement they collected $11,000 over the next few days, which they gave to the Canadian Red Cross for hurricane relief.

Three months later, on December 26, 2004, waking to the news of the tsunami that hit Indonesia, the girls quickly mobilized their resources. With the benefit of the lessons they had learned earlier they spread their message across their community through friends, family, schools and the media. This time the bracelets raised over $100,000 for the Red Cross relief effort.

Shortly after this Deeva was honored to be asked to represent the youth of Toronto by accepting a Bob Marley Day Award for helping out in the Caribbean and was also recognized by the Canadian Red Cross. Since then Deeva has:

- Traveled to India to study diversity, subsequently coordinating a school-wide fundraiser for the Sheela Bal Bhavan Home for girls in India
- Attended the Queenstown GAP (Get Ahead Project) School in South Africa to work on literacy and sustainability
- Spent time in the British Virgin Islands with SAIL Caribbean to

106

work on a conservation project
- Traveled to Nunavut in the Arctic with Students on Ice to study global warming

As if all that was not enough, through her school's community-service initiatives she volunteers for the Best Buddies program, spending time each week with her buddy, Jeremy, a 19-year-old intellectually disabled youth. Through another school program, Horizons, Deeva tutors inner-city youth once a week. Last year she was the head of the Environmental Club at her school and this year is its community-service prefect.

When asked in an interview about her passion for giving back, Deeva said she believes she has a "responsibility to be a good steward of the planet." She said Ontario's requirement that high-school students volunteer 40 hours of community service in order to graduate has helped instill a sense of responsibility and establish strong values in her generation. The indifference of previous generations is a thing of the past. According to Deeva her peers are graduating with an understanding that "success isn't defined by how much money you make, but by what kind of difference you make."

Not bad for a 17 year old. Extraordinary, in fact.

Tonika Morgan

These youth don't all come from economically secure homes. Tonika Morgan is 23 and was born to young, unmarried parents who didn't have the resources to support her. She spent much of her youth in shelters and didn't finish high school. Today Tonika is project manager for Women Moving Forward, a program of the Jane/Finch Community Family Centre, a 30-year-old non-profit in a low-income Toronto neighborhood plagued with crime. Women Moving Forward is dedicated to breaking the cycle of poverty by supporting unemployed single mothers on social assistance to become financially self-sufficient.

Asked why, Tonika explains that she has been compelled to "continue the legacy" for all the people who showed up to help her when she needed it most. She has a mission to thank them by "paying it forward." Tonika has upgraded her education on her own, has worked her way through three years of an undergraduate degree and intends to do an MBA in corporate social responsibility. Her dream is to help connect companies and communities in collaborative efforts.

The Shift

There's even a "do good" pledge form circulating online. It started at Humboldt State University in California, but Manchester College now coordinates the national efforts of the Graduation Pledge Alliance (GPA). Students at well over a hundred colleges and universities have used the pledge at some level. The schools include liberal arts colleges (Whitman and Macalester); state universities (Indiana University and California State University — Chico); and private research universities (Harvard University and University of Pennsylvania). The pledge is also now found at graduate and professional schools, high schools and schools overseas (Taiwan and Australia).

The wording reads:

> I _____ pledge to explore and take into account the social and environmental consequences of any job I consider and will try to improve these aspects of any organizations for which I work.

Added to this ever-increasing social consciousness is the clear message of celebrity role models like Bono, Angelina Jolie, George Clooney, Richard Gere and many others that it's up to us to end poverty and to heal the planet. And then there are the daily visual reminders on the young people's TVs and cellphones that there's a huge amount of unnecessary suffering going on in the world — and that they have the opportunity and abundance to end it. The result is a generation that's starting to ask why.

Gen Xers volunteer more than any other generation in history. The majority of college and university students say that doing volunteer work and making a difference in other people's lives is important to them.

There's been a shift. Their values are different. Their expectations are different. More than paychecks and benefits they're looking for purpose, balance, inspiration, fun, personal growth and an opportunity to make a difference.

And they know what's out there and what's available. The Internet has made corporate culture and karmic comparisons of companies easy for them to conduct. They know who's doing what. They also know that they're in demand. They aren't scared or desperate. They're discerning and patient. They know that the door swings both ways: if one job doesn't meet their needs, there are plenty more out there to consider. As John Izzo and Pam Withers say in *Values Shift*:

> Values are the primary source of energy that drives behavior. Inwardly, we know our values as beliefs. Outwardly they are manifested as behaviors and choices. When our values and work drift apart from one another, we experience a commitment crisis. When they're neatly tied into a bundle, we put our hearts and souls into our work.

The case for corporate responsibility and citizenship has gained huge momentum and is reaching a tipping point. The new employee expects business to play a role in making the world a better place by giving back.

Psychologists have documented that as we age we move away from a focus on "what's in it for me" to a focus on "how can I make a difference?" From taking and having, to giving and legacy. This new generation seems to be making this transition faster than ever — but then it's clear that everything in their world is moving faster than ever.

Exit the Boomers

Meanwhile, members of the baby boom generation, whose impending retirement clock is ticking down to 2011, when it officially begins, intend to stay vital and active but retire early from the traditional work force. In fact a movement toward doing something that has more meaning is already creating an exodus of this cohort from the corporate executive pool.

Jeff Flug

Jeff Flug was managing director and head of North American Institutional Sales at JP Morgan's Investment Bank and managing director of the Fixed Income Division of Goldman Sachs & Co. until a sense began to stir in him that he had a higher purpose. In April 2006, with the support of his family, Jeff took a significant pay cut to become the CEO and executive director of Millennium Promise Alliance. Jeff will lead Millennium Promise as it builds strong alliances between individuals and the private and non-profit sectors. The vision is to eradicate extreme global poverty through the achievement of Millennium development goals.

Paul Alofs

Formerly with Colgate-Palmolive, HMV Music Stores, BMG Music Canada, Disney Stores and MP3.com, Paul Alofs returned to Canada after selling his stock in MP3.com to care for his mother through her ordeal with breast cancer. He is now president and CEO, in Toronto, of the Princess Margaret Hospital Foundation.

"My mother's illness was a life-altering experience," he told the

Globe and Mail shortly after he joined the foundation in 2003. "When I thought about returning to work full time, I looked at a bunch of things in the private sector, but decided I would only do something if my heart was in it."

This move out of the rat race and into the world of the meaningful is a definite trend, Alofs believes. "I think a lot of very talented people are looking at their career, looking for a cause that really motivates them," he says. "The huge attraction of the non-profit sector is that you can work for a cause that's meaningful to you and improve the world in some way."

Jake McArthur

For over 20 years Jake McArthur was president of a number of retail businesses in Canada, including LensCrafters Canada, CDREM Group Inc., Granada TV and Sketchley Cleaners. Throughout a career that involved nurturing and growing businesses as well as people McArthur's attention was consistently drawn to leadership, and also to children — his own and those he encountered in his travels. In 2000 he left his retail career and created a coaching and leadership development practice. The next year, in the wake of the death of his daughter, Erica, in a car accident, he turned to a number of new ways to support others, including volunteering to help children who had suffered loss.

In 2002, combining his passions for leadership and children, McArthur began facilitating leadership development for elementary school students. In 2005 he registered a charitable organization, Leadership Development for Students, as a vehicle to provide what he calls "leadership consciousness" to a wider number of students in both elementary and high schools.

As he told Orenda in an interview, "I've been blessed with a comfortable and exciting life. From a very early age I lived that life believing I was a leader. My work today is helping children adopt that frame for their lives to be the utterly unique leaders only each of them can be. Their lives and their world will be so much better for it."

Mike Russill

After a career at Shell Canada and Petro Canada and as an executive at Suncor, Mike Russell is now president and CEO of World Wildlife Fund Canada. He has this to say, in the Canadian Fundraiser newsletter, about the difference between the two environments:

> In business the leaders are always challenged to motivate their employees, make them want to get up in the morning and come to work because they think it's important and valuable to do the job they've been assigned. Here I found it really wasn't an issue. People in WWF have aligned their lifestyle and their life's work. So when they get out of bed in the morning, they say "hot damn, I'm going to save the world today."

John Wood

John Wood is renowned as the man who took Microsoft into Asia in the 1990s. But he prefers to be known as the man who *left* Microsoft to follow his dream and passion: helping Third World children.

In his book *Leaving Microsoft to Change the World*, Wood recounts how he felt trapped between his all-consuming career at Microsoft and his desire to make a difference in the world. It took a trekking trip to Nepal to show him the way out of that trap. Visiting a school in a remote part of the country he was shocked by the lack of books in its library. At that moment he put into motion plans for a new organization, Room to Read. He returned to the school himself with thousands of books on the back of a yak. Since then Room to Read has donated more than 1.2 million books, established more than 2,600 libraries and 200 schools and sent 1,700 girls to school on scholarship. As Wood says in his book:

> If you are thinking about making some adjustments in your life to allow you to help change the world, my heartfelt recommendation is not to spend too much time thinking about it. If there is something out there that you want to do to make the world a better place, don't focus on the obstacles. Don't ask for permission. Just dive in.

These people have filled the holes in their hearts. Their stories are of ah-ha moments and life-changing decisions. However, we don't have to leave our work and businesses to make a difference; we just need to transform our workplaces with inspiration here and now. By harnessing the power of a corporate philanthropy program we can create workplace environments that make our values sing.

The shrinking pool of aging employees, who are looking to make a difference and leave a legacy, combined with the new generation of employees, who are looking to stand for something in the work they do, is creating urgency for business. A collective consciousness in the workforce is demanding that businesses step up and focus on creating good corporate karma. Any company that turns a blind eye to this critical component of attracting and retaining good talent is going to wake up one day and ask, "Where have all our people gone?"

9

From Collecting
to Collaborating
The Non-profit Message

It is in giving that we receive.
— ST. FRANCIS OF ASSISSI

James E. Austin of the Harvard Business School writes in his book *The Collaboration Challenge*:

> Beyond learning how to collaborate each partner gains specific valuable skills and knowledge. A nonprofit, for example, might develop marketing, financial or business planning skills; its business partner might acquire knowledge of a target group of consumers, new organizational or employee motivational methods or community relations skills. Employees engaged in community service projects might hone their leadership or team-work capabilities. The mutual learning benefits of collaboration are many and represent another payoff from partnering.

It's not easy out there for the non-profits, or so some say. The call for their services is probably greater in our society and our world than ever before. The competition for funding is greater, too, because there are more and more charities competing for a smaller piece of the corporate pie. Dave Phillips, president of Children's Hunger Fund™, summarized the challenge in this way in an Orenda interview: "Corporate margins are smaller, mergers and acquisitions greatly affect a charity's ability to craft new relationships, and in some cases long-term relationships vaporize overnight as new leadership comes in with a different agenda."

As we've discovered, however, great corporate-cause partnerships are about much more than giving and receiving money. They are about meshing missions, resources and skills to create a win-win-win — for the company, the non-profit and the world.

That the new philanthropy model is starting to spread through the business world is good news for non-profits. The evolution of business strategy to include community giving means that more and more funding will be provided to the non-profit world from companies of all sizes, as businesses design their giving programs and choose relevant non-profit partners. And that funding, if integrated with a strategic philanthropy program, will set up long-term, regular income, as opposed to a check today, nothing tomorrow.

The new model does require non-profits to understand what companies are looking for in these partnerships and to meet those needs. For the non-profits the good news is that there is more sustainable funding available. The more challenging news for non-profits is that they must be able to show up as a corporate-ready partner. No more hands out simply saying, "Please, sir, I want some more." Now it's about reciprocity.

If you are a non-profit the most important consideration is to be absolutely clear about what you are able and not able to provide. It can be so tempting for you to say you can or will do something that the company is asking if you think it will lead to a financial gain for you. We caution you not to make promises you cannot keep.

One of our clients manufactures a high-quality protein supplement. Prior to working with us they had been supporting an organization dedicated to the prevention and treatment of child abuse. They wanted to design a program for their employees to not only support their charity with cash contributions but also purchase their protein supplement for children in the charity's residential treatment facilities.

In their initial conversation with the charity they were told that this was great, that it would be wonderful for the children to have the benefit of this supplement to help them physically as they were healing emotionally. After the program had been rolled out, however, the charity came back to say they would not be able to accept the supplement due to federal restrictions on what could and could not be fed to the children in their care.

This was a huge blow to our client, and they had to quickly disable their employee program. It was a lesson in making sure you can do what you say you can do.

Tips for Non-profits

By turning the lessons from the previous chapters inside out we can help you as a non-profit know what companies are looking for.

Relevance

Most businesses will look for a non-profit focusing on community work that is somehow connected and relevant to the work they are doing. This should be helpful to you as you think about who may be good corporate partners.

Look at your cause category and identify the industries for which you would make a relevant fit.

Connection

Business leaders are not just looking for someone with their hand out. They're looking for a partner they can connect with. Just as we advise the company that the CEO needs to be the champion of this collaboration and giving intent, so we advise that the CEO or executive director of the non-profit needs to be the liaison with the corporation. Show the company that this partnership is important. Show an interest in their business and how they can work with you to make a difference. Be a partner that wants to be part of the planning process for their giving program. One that "shows up" and is present for them even after the check has been written, and before the next check is expected.

In *The Collaboration Challenge* Austin writes:

> The engagement of and relationships between top leaders of the corporation and the non-profit largely determine the acceptance and vigor of the collaboration ... Creating opportunities for interaction and service engagement by employees at all levels in both organizations fosters personal relationships and connection with the cause.

Participation

Many businesses are looking for organizations that can provide hands-on opportunities, organizing volunteer time for employees. Be clear about how an individual or a group of employees will be able to participate in your work. Are there "roll up your sleeves and work" opportunities? Are there skills or expertise that your partner could contribute to the organization? How can you provide them with the "juice" that brings their commitment to life for them?

Customization/Branding

Businesses pride themselves on being unique. Rather than suggesting a cookie-cutter giving program to your corporate partner be prepared to customize a program with them. Together you may create a brand for the partnership with a unique look and feel that distinguishes their connection with you from the programs of your other corporate partners. Rather than having a broad description of where their efforts are being targeted, be specific and focused with their project. That way, rather than saying, "We're supporting abc charity," they can say, "We are funding this specific project with abc charity."

Accountability

Be prepared to report back to your corporate partner, letting them know exactly where their funds and contributions are going and the difference they're making. Gone are the days when the contributions you receive are yours to do with as you please. If you've committed your partner's funds to a certain project, make sure that's where they're going and report back on the results. Everyone understands that there are administrative costs involved with charity work. Be clear and direct about how their funds will be distributed.

Organization

It's important for you to have an organizational structure in place, particularly when it comes to volunteer efforts. If a group of employees is showing up somewhere make sure their time is well organized and spent. Travel, food, accommodation and supplies are all things that you may need to organize in order to facilitate an inspiring experience. The quality of the experience will contribute to ongoing enthusiasm for the project.

Administration

If employees of a company are making cash contributions be prepared to provide tax receipts. By working closely with your corporate partner you should be able to design a reporting system that will provide you with the information you need to issue tax receipts. Time and in-kind contributions may also need to be accounted for, so make sure you have a clear understanding of the kind of administration your partner is expecting from you.

Communication

The success of your program, which will directly impact its longevity as well as recurring income to fund it, rests largely on your ability to communicate effectively with your partner regarding the work you are doing. Most companies have monthly or bimonthly newsletters, blogs, Websites, events and other communication tools. You must always be prepared to provide information to and through these tools. By showing up for their communications proactively, rather than waiting to be asked for information, you will give them the most important reason to stay in partnership with you: inspiration and good corporate karma.

Partnership

The true integration of company and cause becomes evident when the conversation moves from "us and them" to "we."

What the Non-profits Have Learned

Children's Hunger Fund™ (CHF) has been in a strategic partnership with USANA Health Sciences for the past five years. Here's what Dave Phillips, president of CHF, said about that partnership, in an interview with Orenda:

> *How has CHF as an organization benefited from the partnership?*
> Our relationship with USANA is now five years old, and during that time USANA has contributed more than $3 million in cash and in-kind product to our programs.
>
> The relationship with USANA is unique in that they are a network marketing company. USANA corporate has provided

a mechanism for all of its independent distributors to help CHF financially, by contributing through their monthly autoship program. This mechanism has given CHF access to thousands of personal relationships within the company. As a result many contribute personally to CHF; some volunteer their time to us in a variety of ways; and others have conducted fundraisers in their local communities, which further benefits CHF. CHF support and name recognition have grown dramatically in new communities across the United States and Canada.

What lessons has CHF learned about corporate partnership?
As with most things in life the best things come through relationships. The USANA partnership has flourished, in my opinion, because we have been given the forum to engage individuals within the company on a personal basis. I have been given the opportunity to speak at conventions, which allows many to hear my heart and become engaged with us on a personal level. I have also learned that corporate partnerships must be a win-win for all involved. Charities can become guilty of looking at a corporate partner purely from a selfish basis. Anytime you can create a relationship that increases market share for the corporate partner, increases sales or has some other tangible or intangible benefit for the corporation, the more entrenched the charity can become in the relationship. Donor loyalty will increase proportionately as well.

Learning from our past, our approach to corporate partnerships has changed dramatically. Rather than simply asking corporate partners to help us we now take the approach of crafting a proposal where we try to outline the tangible benefits for the partner if they engage us in a relationship. A charity also needs to remain flexible to the changing needs and trends of the corporate partner.

And here's what Emily Franson, director of community outreach for Choice Humanitarian, said to us, also in an interview:

How has the corporate partnership with Spectrum Health Care benefited Choice Humanitarian?
Partnering with corporations has turned out to be a great program for our organization. When it comes to global poverty, the first step to solving the problem is to increase awareness. Partnering with a company allows us to connect to a wider audience, giving us a greater reach for our message. The second step is inviting people to join us in making a difference. The corporate partnership allows us to extend that invitation to a broad employee base. Finally, the Spectrum partnership is generating recurring income, allowing a village to travel the path to sustainable development and giving us the resources to provide them with the necessities to get there.

What lessons have you learned about corporate partnership?
The program works best when certain key factors are in place:

1. Buy-in at the top. You need the CEO to fully support the program. If the employees see the CEO as a champion of the program, they are more likely to support it
2. Company *and* employees need to contribute. In order to create a sense of team and community, both need to be involved in the project. Otherwise the employees can feel they are pitted against the cause or the company
3. People need to be personally involved. As the charity you have to make their contributions come to life for them. It's about emotion. Until you can show them how they are making a difference few will cross the threshold to truly give

4. A launch of the program is crucial. We learned this with Spectrum Health Care. Of all the partnerships to that point Spectrum was the most successful because of the launch. There is power and momentum when people are together, outside of work, celebrating something good. That momentum can then translate to the rest of the company

5. Ongoing updates are crucial. People want to know what's going on and feel connected. Emotional visuals, photos and stories that they can relate to are key

6. Keep it simple. Keep the barriers to entry low

7. Look at the corporate communication style and culture and build the program around it. Is it best to produce print, digital info, quick e-mails, voicemail messages, blogs, employee meetings?

8. Manage expectations and have a letter of agreement or understanding from the start

9. Be patient. As the partnership grows the benefits for both the company and you will become evident and develop with time

There's no doubt about it. If non-profits and corporations can work together to understand and respect the dynamics between them, focus on mutual goals and objectives and manage expectations and work collaboratively, they can collectively contribute great things to our lives and our communities.

From Collecting to Collaborating

There's a big difference between fundraising and strategic philanthropic partnerships. Usually fundraisers show up to existing and potential corporate partners with a presentation of who they are and what they need. Fundraisers now need to show up asking questions and hearing the answers. Fundamentally, non-profits must become masters of the sales process. They must find out what the company needs and then show them how they can give it to them.

The very first meeting between the company and the cause should be a "discovery process" for both.

The company needs to know who you are, what you do and how you do it. *And* they also need to know that you are there to partner with them to help them meet their needs.

You, meanwhile, need to know who the company is, what they do, how they do it. Do your homework before you meet and find out what giving they have done in the past and what they are hoping to accomplish with their philanthropy program.

Ask questions:

- What giving programs have you done in the past?
- What has worked? What hasn't worked?
- What are you looking to accomplish with your giving program?
- Are you hoping to inspire the workplace?
- Are you hoping to leave a legacy?
- Are you looking to improve your brand reputation and awareness?
- Are you looking for hands-on opportunities for your employees?
- How do you plan to communicate your program?
- Are you planning to contribute cash? Product? Services? Skills?
- How will you know if this program is successful?

By considering these questions you will be able to customize a presentation for them that will show how a partnership with you can help them get what they're looking for. A win-win-win — for the company, the non-profit and for the people whose lives are being changed.

PARTNERSHIP CHECKLIST

- *Relevance*
- *Connection*
- *Participation*
- *Customization*
- *Accountability*
- *Organization*
- *Administration*
- *Communication*

(10)

Walking the Talk
The Pathfinders

History will be our judge, but what's written is up to us ...
We can choose to shift the responsibility,
or we can choose to shift the paradigm.
— BONO

You can't learn to drive by reading a book. You need to watch and be taught by good drivers. The same is true of setting up a corporate philanthropy program. While the previous chapters have outlined the *why* and *how* of strategic corporate philanthropy, this chapter allows you to watch how inspiring companies have taken these principles and turned sound theory into amazing practice.

The companies we've chosen come from different industries and range from very small to Fortune 500. Each one has its own unique approach to company giving. The message they all have in common is clear: Strategic corporate philanthropy is just plain good for business.

ERICSSON: Supporting Disaster Relief Through Coordinated Communications

Ericsson's Expertise, Equipment and Employees Are at the Ready

Within a few days of the devastating tsunami that hit South Asia on December 26, 2004, a team from Ericsson Indonesia was close to the epicenter with technical expertise, 10 radio-base stations and hundreds of mobile phones. Ericsson Response built an emergency telecommunications service in the disaster zone that facilitated essential communications between local and international relief agencies. While this event will always be remembered as catastrophic, there is no doubt that dedicated organizations like Ericsson Response helped ease suffering and save lives.

Communications are critical to the efficient allocation of resources in a relief effort. Ericsson is a world-leading provider of telecommunications equipment and related services. It has a long tradition of giving support in disaster situations, with a presence in many countries for over 100 years. But before Response there was neither a cohesive strategy nor the leadership to develop one. Ericsson Response was established by Ericsson in 1999 to create a more efficient way to coordinate international telecommunications in these disaster situations.

The initiative for Ericsson Response originated as a corporate citizenship activity for the Ericsson Group by a few employees working at Ericsson Canada. A study of stakeholders was commissioned to help it understand internal and external expectations of the company in terms of corporate citizenship — an issue that was not common in Europe at the time. The study found a good fit between expectations, the company's offering and the support of humanitarian relief through telecommunications. While the company had always contributed to disaster relief with telecom support, it was usually through local business groups aiding local customers.

The decision to move forward with Ericsson Response came from the top: the CEO Management Team. Dag Nielsen, the first and current director of Ericsson Response, had an established network within the United Nations (UN) and International Federation of Red Cross and Red Crescent Societies (IFRC). By integrating his network with company experience and resources, Ericsson Response was born.

Today the program has evolved considerably and reports in to the VP of Customer Support and Ericsson Response, who continues to oversee its operations. Steering committees have been set up from time to time, but the daily coordination, training and communications are carried out by three full-time employees, in addition to the VP of Customer Support. The decision to move Ericsson Response into a key operational part of the company has streamlined and improved Ericsson Response's ability to react quickly in times of disaster.

Key to responding effectively to a disaster is having the right people with the right skills available at a moment's notice. Ericsson Response has identified the human resources needed to fulfill its mandate. Internal applications are screened against these needs. Successful applicants obtain the commitment of their manager to free them up for a minimum of one month per year. Once all this has been done they attend a four-day training course that involves the UN and the IFRC. The classroom education covers international and humanitarian law, how non-governmental organizations operate, security issues and finally how the system works within

Ericsson. One full day of the program is a simulated disaster exercise. According to Dag, "Some people say it's the best course they take in any category."

Many companies in the telecommunications industry contribute to disaster-relief efforts. Ericsson is different, according to Dag, because it "has a disaster preparedness program. We have the equipment in place and the people trained in different countries. We know what and who is where. We can move into action quickly."

Through the homepage that every employee sees when they boot up their computer, as well as the company's intranet site, newspaper and presentations at internal meetings, Ericsson's over 50,000 employees in 140 countries are kept abreast of the organization's work. Each year the management team reviews how Ericsson Response performed relative to established goals, but it is the enthusiasm of employees that is the true measure of its success. A great deal of informal feedback indicates that employees value it highly.

Dag sees the program as useful not only in satisfying current employees but also in attracting the best prospective employees. "The values of young people today dictate that we must be the right company — not just offer the right salary," he says. "We think that by having these kinds of programs we are more attractive to the type of people we want to employ."

The company's commitment to Ericsson Response is long term. Even during more turbulent times, when other programs were being cut, Ericsson Response was not. "Our employees and managers like it," says Dag. "It injects pride into the company. It is good for morale."

HASBRO: Giving the Gift of a Smile

For Hasbro and Employees, Philanthropy Is Child's Play

With products like Monopoly, Candy Land and My Little Pony, Hasbro Inc. brightens millions of lives every day. But Hasbro doesn't stop there. With their mission of "Giving the Gift of Hope, Play and a Helpful Hand" the company strives for a higher measure of success through a multifaceted philanthropy program. The joy of Hasbro's child-focused giving is felt across North America and around the globe. Karen Davis, vice president of Community Relations, says it is not just the company that makes a difference. "Our employees donate their time toward many programs. It generates a common sense of pride in the company."

In his foreword to *Compassionate Capitalism*, Hasbro chairman Alan Hassenfeld writes: "We believe in living charity in my family, where we get out and participate personally, and we've tried to pass on that commitment to our company." Hassenfeld, grandson of the company's founder, promotes this family tradition of giving back through the company's philanthropic programs. Hasbro encourages and helps employees to get involved in their community. They communicate volunteering opportunities in their area, customize department volunteer programs and offer four hours of paid volunteer time each month.

One of Hasbro's longest-standing national philanthropic efforts has been directed toward Boundless Playgrounds, which has created 100 playgrounds since it began in 1998. The company has supported this non-profit since its inception, joining them in encouraging communities to build playgrounds where children of all abilities can play together. The company has also supported the construction of two of its own Boundless Playgrounds given to children in their operating areas.

Hasbro also gives employees an opportunity to experience the satisfaction of actively making the world better for children by physically helping to build the playgrounds. This unifies the company. Recently Hasbro's Playskool brand presented a contest to "Win a Boundless Playground" — the creation and cost of which will be taken on entirely by the Playskool brand with support from GameTime.

Hassenfeld insists that a company should support their community not only because it is the right thing to do but also because it is the profitable thing to do. A strong bottom line requires strong communities, he says. After all it is in the community that employees, customers and other supporters are found. Being recognized as a contributing member to the community makes individuals, organizations and shareholders keen to associate with you. "I believe that the competitive advantage you gain from being a caring and sharing company is significant," he adds.

Hasbro is certainly caring and sharing. They support their loyal community and provide national and international support through strategic partnerships. Under the direction of CEO Al Verrecchia they make generous financial and product donations to orphanages and hospitals — especially the Hasbro Children's Hospital in Rhode Island, where the company is based. With Operation Smile they help provide medical aid to children in China with facial deformities who typically would not receive treatment. Through World Vision the company is helping AIDS orphans in Zambia, providing support to 40 schools where the orphans are educated and providing in-kind support as well.

Hasbro goes beyond games and toys to bring smiles to the faces of children with special challenges. Their strategic approach to philanthropy — one that is aligned with the company's commercial efforts and encourages employee participation — has resulted in many awards. But recognition is not their objective. What they are really after are those smiles.

THE HOME DEPOT: Bringing New Meaning to Community Building

The Home Depot Hammers Home the Spirit of Volunteerism

At The Home Depot the tag line "You Can Do It. We Can Help" is more than just an advertising slogan or a message aimed at consumers with a do-it-yourself inclination. With over 3,000 stores and 355,000 employees The Home Depot is committed to using its resources to help make a difference in communities across the US, Canada and Mexico.

The company's volunteer program, Team Depot, encourages employees to roll up their sleeves and build, rebuild and refurbish physical spaces that are key to creating thriving communities. And employees don't do it alone. The program is built with their "You Can Do It. We Can Help" mentality, engaging community members, family members and associates to join in the spirit of community and work together. Also, Team Depot sees the building of community spaces as a way to transform lives. Their credo is rooted in the belief that given the right spaces and places, people such as children, those in need of low-income housing and the disabled will reach their greatest potential.

"Giving back to our communities is not only a responsibility," says former CEO Bob Nardelli, "it is part of doing business at The Home Depot." In fact giving back is so central to the company that it is one of the eight values under which the company operates. Nardelli acknowledges the valuable connection between volunteerism and employee engagement when he states that "the kind of associate who has a passion for helping his or her community is the kind of associate who is serious about helping customers."

To date employees have built homes for Habitat for Humanity, sent associates to provide hands-on rebuilding support in natural disaster and crisis situations and renovated over 20,000 homes for the elderly and the disabled. One of the company's strongest partnerships is with KaBOOM!, a non-profit organization with a vision to give every child in America access to a great place to play. As the founding partner in KaBOOM!, The Home Depot has stepped up to the plate, mobilizing more than 40,000 volunteers to build or improve more than 500 community playgrounds, skate parks and sports fields across North America.

As in all good partnerships The Home Depot and KaBOOM! share a core vision. Both believe that strength comes through collaboration. KaBOOM! does more than engage employees of The Home Depot in building playgrounds. They bring together local children and community members to participate. And they do more than build play spaces: they provide resources for communities that want to create playgrounds of their own.

Based on the success of the partnership to date The Home Depot has made a commitment to create and refurbish over 1,000 playgrounds in the next three years. Doing this will require an investment of $25 million, combined with over one million hours of volunteer time. It's a tall order, but given the company's track record, there is no doubt Team Depot can get the job done.

It's obvious that Team Depot loves to build things — it's the skill set they bring. "When you look into the eyes of these associates, many times it becomes emotional," says Nardelli. "Some of these saintly men and women who devote their lives to inner cities — you know you have touched their lives."

In fact the success of the KaBOOM! partnership inspired The Home Depot to make an unprecedented commitment to supplying vitally needed volunteer elbow grease. In honor of the company's

25th anniversary, in 2004, The Home Depot initiated its first ever Week of Service. From September 27 to October 4 close to 35,000 employees, along with 17,000 family members, gave 200,000 hours of volunteer service to 1,600 community-based projects in the US, Canada, Mexico and the company's sourcing office in China.

The Home Depot partners KaBOOM! and Hands On Network helped identify improvement projects that ranged from building playgrounds and creating walking trails to painting school murals and landscaping parks. And The Home Depot employees, partners and their families gathered to share in a truly special week that Michelle Nunn, president and CEO of Hands On Network, called "an incredible event [that] truly symbolized the power of volunteers in action."

The groundbreaking nature of The Home Depot's commitment to community has been widely acknowledged by both the non-profit and corporate community. The Points of Light Foundation and the Committee to Encourage Corporate Philanthropy have both lauded the relationship between The Home Depot and KaBOOM! as a startling model of non-profit/corporate collaboration. The key to success for The Home Depot has been its authentic belief in collaboration — with non-profits, community members, employees, suppliers and others — to create better places to play, live and gather together.

LUXOTTICA GROUP: Crafting a Focused Philanthropy Program

Luxottica Group Gives the Gift of Sight

Business success stories were a rare occurrence in the early 1980s. But out of the recession came an ambitious exception. LensCrafters revolutionized the vision-care industry in 1983 by offering one-stop shopping for eyeglasses in a retail rather than medical environment. By putting the optometrist's office, frame dispensary and manufacturing lab under one roof, LensCrafters was able to offer eyeglasses "in about an hour," and the concept was an instant success. Not long after, the company spun business success into philanthropic success.

Focusing on what it knew best LensCrafters began donating new glasses to needy people selected by local schools and charitable agencies. In 1988 it initiated a program in conjunction with Lions Clubs International to collect used glasses for distribution abroad. The young company realized that millions of people around the world suffer from poor vision simply because they lack resources or access to the eyeglasses most of us take for granted. As more and more employees experienced firsthand the power of delivering the gift of sight, a passion for helping others took hold in the business, along with the belief that clear vision is a basic right, not a luxury. By 1993 Give the Gift of Sight Foundation, a 501c3 operating charity, was established.

Give the Gift of Sight has grown to encompass a family of charitable vision-care programs that, since 1991, have provided free eye exams, new and recycled glasses, vision screenings and fittings and adjustments to more than five million people around the world. LensCrafters is now part of Luxottica Group, along with Pearle Vision, Sunglass Hut, Sears Optical, BJ's and Target Optical. Luxottica Group, the high-end Italy-based eyeglass frame manufacturer, is a global leader in eyewear, with nearly 5,500 optical and sun retail stores mainly in North America and Asia-Pacific. Luxottica Group has embraced and expanded the Gift of Sight program — setting a goal to help seven million people by 2008.

Give the Gift of Sight began small. After collecting and delivering used glasses to Lions Clubs International for several years, the program in 1991 mounted its first international mission trip to Costa Rica to distribute recycled glasses to people without access to eye care. Between 1991 and 2006 Gift of Sight has executed 117 missions to 27 developing countries, helping more than two million recipients see their world more clearly.

The partnership with Lions Clubs International has flourished. Lions districts worldwide co-sponsor Gift of Sight international missions. They identify up to 30,000 people with visual and financial need for each mission, transport them to the clinic and handle some logistics for the team. Doctors affiliated with Luxottica perform eye exams, and technicians match recipients with recycled glasses that exactly or nearly match their prescriptions. Each two-week trip helps from 25,000 to 30,000 people in eight clinic days. Sixteen international missions were executed in 2006 alone to Mexico, Panama, Romania, Ecuador, China, Honduras, Paraguay, Mali and Chile.

In a parallel North American program Luxottica Group doctors and employees donate free eye exams and new glasses at home through in-store and outreach programs. Two 40-foot vans, called SeeMore and Iris, deliver exams and new glasses to children in remote locations. Stores donate more than 100,000 pairs of new glasses annually through voucher programs and an annual day of giving. On the first Tuesday of December all Luxottica

North American retail locations celebrate Hometown Day by opening early to provide free eye exams and new glasses to about 20,000 people selected by local agencies.

Luxottica employees deliver Gift of Sight programs on company and personal time. The company supports Gift of Sight participation on work time because of its proven ability to develop employee pride, recruit and retain top talent, offer powerful team-building opportunities and provide meaningful leadership training and diversity experiences. And as Luxottica Group has expanded, Gift of Sight has helped build bridges among the new brands.

Involvement with Gift of Sight begins at the store level where employees are empowered to help the needy in their communities. Those who seek to do more step up to serve as a Gift of Sight Store Captain, then a regional Gift of Sight Captain and/or coordinator of a regional Vision Van mission. Finally, they are ready to apply for a coveted spot on an international or North American mission. Team members are selected based on involvement in and leadership of local activities. The volunteer hierarchy and goal of being selected for a two-week, all-expenses-paid experience of a lifetime (on payroll!), helps fuel program leadership.

Capturing and sharing heartwarming stories of people seeing clearly for the first time has also fueled program growth. Most employees can relate stories about the mother in Kenya who cried when she saw her baby for the first time or the tough, glum-faced Chicago schoolboy who broke out in a huge smile when he first noticed leaves on trees. Sharing that magic moment when a recipient sees clearly for the first time benefits the Gift of Sight volunteer as much as the recipient. "The program offers instant gratification over and over. What can be better than that?" asks program founder Susan Knobler.

These stories have become part of the company's folklore. Progress toward annual Gift of Sight goals is shared and celebrated quarterly alongside corporate business goals. Through newsletters, videos, meetings and word of mouth all employees learn how millions of people worldwide lack basic vision-care services and what a difference the company makes by providing it.

Give the Gift of Sight leverages Luxottica Group's core competencies to help people see and help employees find higher meaning in their work. Adds Knobler, "Our philanthropy has elevated the way we feel about our business. We're not just selling glasses; we're changing people's lives."

M·A·C Cosmetics: Being Glam for Life

M·A·C Cosmetics Employees, Artists and Retailers Unite in Support of Those Living with HIV/AIDS

The world has been affected by AIDS for more than a quarter of a century. It is the fourth leading cause of death globally. Fourteen million children have been orphaned by the disease. The statistics are devastating. The picture is dismal. But there are also images of hope and inspirational stories of people working together to make life better for individuals living with HIV/AIDS and educate society to limit its transmission. The M·A·C AIDS Fund is at the center of many such stories.

When M·A·C Cosmetics chose HIV/AIDS as their cause for corporate giving it raised more than a few eyebrows. A company that traded on fantasy and beauty was choosing a cause that was harshly real and decidedly unglamorous. But for M·A·C Cosmetics and its employees the cause was, and is, very personal. Some employees are HIV positive. Most employees have experience with the disease either through family or friends. All understand the needs of those living with HIV/AIDS, thanks to regular, company-wide seminars. Employees wholeheartedly support the fund's mission to lend financial assistance for food, housing, medicine and education to those living with the disease. Their commitment is so great that the fund has been called the "heart and soul" of the company.

The fund was personal from the start. It was founded by Frank Toskan and Frank Angelo, co-founders of the company. In 1994, as the AIDS epidemic spread and began to impact the fashion and entertainment world, the men searched for a way to deal with their personal sense of loss. Encouraged by M·A·C employees they decided to make HIV/AIDS organizations the beneficiaries of the company's charitable giving.

Today more than $65 million has been raised by the fund, primarily through the company's VIVA GLAM lipstick line. There are now five VIVA GLAM colors. A new color is launched each year by top personalities from the arts, music and entertainment communities. Each celebrity develops their own unique message concerning HIV/AIDS and the importance of supporting the cause by purchasing VIVA GLAM lipstick. Pamela Anderson, Elton John, RuPaul, k.d. lang, Linda Evangelista and Boy George are just a few of the celebrities who have spoken for the product.

While celebrity support of the fund has been important to its success, the involvement of all M·A·C employees, including the makeup artists at M·A·C stores and partner retailers, is fundamental to the daily revenue generated by VIVA GLAM lipstick. However, employees do more than develop, package and sell the lipstick. Craig Cichy, manager of the fund, says, "It's amazing the number of activities they are involved in."

Across North America M·A·C teams are formed by employees to participate in AIDS walks, raising money for community-based HIV/AIDS services. The fund matches all donations raised by M·A·C teams on these walks as a way to get funding directly to the communities of M·A·C employees while raising local awareness of HIV/AIDS.

Through the company's Good Spirits program M·A·C makeup artists offer one-on-one support to those living with HIV/AIDS. Good Spirits is modeled on the American Cancer Society's Look Good ... Feel Better campaign. It involves M·A·C makeup artists volunteering at AIDS organizations to teach those living with HIV/AIDS how to use makeup to enhance their appearance and minimize problems resulting from the illness or medication regimens.

M·A·C employees are active in many community activities. Cichy is inspired by their fundraising efforts. "And they don't even tell us sometimes. We'll just receive an envelope of checks from an event organized by M·A·C employees that we weren't aware of."

The M·A·C AIDS Fund has been honored with numerous awards internationally for its commitment to supporting the millions of people impacted by HIV/AIDS. For M·A·C Cosmetics HIV/AIDS is not a cause of the moment. It is a commitment that permeates every aspect of what they do and how they do it. From R&D to merchandising, everyone is involved. In Cichy's words, the fund "is woven into the fabric of the company."

ROBERT KENT PHOTOGRAPHY: Assembling and Acting

One Photographer Mobilizes Many More

Altruistic enthusiasm and the long light of June 21, 2006, energized the photographers, models, hair and makeup artists in the first ever Summer Solstice Shoot for the Compassionate Eye Foundation. The event resulted in the selection of 300 images by Getty Images, which is expected to generate significant funding for the foundation over the next few years. It is the fruit of an ambitious and generous philanthropic effort initiated by Robert Kent and supporters. It is a story of caring in action.

The Compassionate Eye Foundation was built from the heart. Upon returning from trips to South Africa and Cambodia, Robert was feeling grateful for the abundance in his life. He felt it was "time to make a difference" and give back. With the support and guidance of a few friends he assembled the people who would make the foundation a reality and started planning.

Robert learned that there were three basic requirements for a successful foundation: workers, wisdom and wealth. He was prepared for the work. He could recruit and develop the wisdom. Wealth was the challenge. The foundation started very small. Robert put much of his own money into the startup costs. A fundraising dinner held at his home raised $2,000. Small donations from family and friends filled in a few gaps. But something substantial was required. Robert saw the opportunity within his own industry.

As a photographer with an impressive 21-year career Robert spends 50% of his time on custom photography shoots for specific advertising clients. He licenses the other 50% of his work to Getty Images as stock photography. It was in this latter business model that Robert saw his chance to generate wealth for the foundation, by winning the support of other photographers to create stock photography and directing the royalty receipts to the foundation.

On June 21, 12 photographers and crews volunteered their time for studio and location shoots. A variety of locations were used, including the beach, hotels and supermarkets. Crews in New Mexico and Thailand participated, but most of the shoots were in the Vancouver area. A dinner party was held at the end of the day celebrating the joy of collaboration and the potential of their efforts. Robert's editor from Getty Images had never seen anything like it. It was the first time in his 20 years of industry experience that he had been involved in a shoot for a higher cause.

Based in British Columbia the foundation is dedicated to supporting developing nations through educational initiatives. The focus of their effort is currently on Comitancillo, a very poor municipality in the northwest part of Guatemala. In March 2006, believing that education could help address the community's unemployment problem, the foundation purchased land for a new school. Since then $10,000 has been donated for the cost of material and labor for its construction. Further donations are planned to equip the school. This is the type of giving back that Robert Kent and the Compassionate Eye Foundation are so passionate about.

The Summer Solstice Shoot was a great success. There was more interest than organizers could handle. Now that the foundation has the systems and contracts in place, the event can grow. Many more photographers and crews are expected to participate in future years.

The desire to make a difference and innovative thinking have resulted in a bright future for the foundation. Robert expects that in five years it will be a multi-million-dollar organization. He is bracing himself for a major change in his life. Now that he has learned that so many are willing, he will continue to assemble supporters and act.

SPECTRUM HEALTH CARE: Inspiring Employees Through Philanthropy

Determined to Transform Health Services in a Guatemalan Village, Spectrum Employees Undergo Their Own Transformation

Community is a vision reinforced by action driven by common purpose. Strong communities — those actively pursuing a common purpose — grow in amazing ways. This is the belief on which Spectrum Health Care based its new approach to corporate giving. The company decided to focus on supporting one community. In doing so they also hoped to strengthen the Spectrum Health Care community. Less than a year into their strategic philanthropy initiative the benefits were being realized by the Guatemalan village they adopted and by their own employees.

Spectrum has a large number of nurses and personal support workers providing care in homes across the Greater Toronto Area. Due to the nature of their work these front-line employees rarely get together. Lori Lord, Spectrum's Chief Operating Officer, wanted this group to enjoy the same sense of community that employees at most firms enjoy. Her solution dovetailed with the company's giving plan. It was to involve them in a common purpose that would be inspirational.

With our help at Orenda Lori led the company in its new approach to giving — one that engaged employees and encouraged participation. Its merit was immediately obvious. After the announcement of the initiative one employee wrote: "I can't tell you the excitement I have felt since this has unfolded. I will fulfill one of my dreams thanks to Spectrum Health Care. We both have the same agenda."

The first step in the Spectrum initiative was the selection of a charity by a committee of employees and management. Given the company's focus on health it seemed appropriate that their philanthropic efforts should also be health related. They decided their efforts would be international, since Canadians are already relatively well served by their health-care system. With an eye to sustainability the company sought projects that guided a community to self-sufficiency. They were concerned that contributions would be well managed — the charitable organization they chose would have to be experienced and responsible. After narrowing the many options to three, proposals were reviewed in detail. Spectrum selected Choice Humanitarian as its charitable organization and Xalibe, Guatemala, as its community to support.

Xalibe is a village high in the mountains of Guatemala. Speaking a dialect of the ancient Mayan empire, the Xalibe community of about 35 families suffers from the collapse of their coffee industry, the lack of a new vision for income and, consequently, extreme poverty. Death in childbirth, from malnutrition and from other manageable causes is common. The village needed help setting priorities and developing new skills and resources. Choice Humanitarian had people in Guatemala with the right experience to help the community on behalf of Spectrum.

Spectrum management financed the completion of a water system for the village — a basic need for good health — even before the program began. Water was the only drink served at the event that launched the program. The significance of this became clear as the evening progressed.

The launch was an evening of food, fun and serious business. Through presentations by Spectrum Health Care management and Choice Humanitarian, employees learned about the needs and plans for Xalibe. First a basic medical station would be built and supplied. Then a few people in the village would be trained to improve the well-being of the entire community. As the importance of what could be achieved became clear, the energy in the room grew. The comment of one nurse reflected the feelings of many: "This project gives us the chance to stretch out our hand to our fellow man and make the world a better place." Enthusiasm was also actively demonstrated when triple the anticipated financial support for the initiative was pledged.

The Xalibe strategic philanthropy project has brought the Spectrum Health Care employee community together working toward a common purpose. To keep them connected a blog on the village itself has been set up. Communication updates are ongoing through e-mails, voicemail and the company newsletter. Additional events are being planned. Each year a group of employees will have an opportunity to earn a trip to the village on behalf of everyone at Spectrum to view the results of employee efforts.

Key to the success of Spectrum's strategic philanthropy initiative is employee ownership. The project is now in their hands. While Spectrum's management will support their objectives, it is up to the employees — as a community — to carry it into the future.

TIMBERLAND: Becoming Good Corporate Citizens and Committed Employees

Timberland Enjoys Many Benefits by Supporting Volunteerism

In January 2006 the Timberland Company was selected by *Fortune* magaine for the ninth year in a row as one of the 100 Best Companies to Work For. In May of that year it received a 100 Best Corporate Citizens award from *Business Ethics* magazine. Recognition in these two categories highlights the important relationship between corporate citizenship and corporate morale. Timberland president and CEO Jeffrey Swartz says that being recognized in both categories "is a humbling affirmation that we're following the right path," one that "strengthens our commitment to do more."

It is not just employee satisfaction and good corporate citizenship that go hand in hand. At a 2005 conference on philanthropy Swartz connected the growth of Timberland's community involvement with the company's profits. The fact of growing profits "is not a factor of my brilliant, strategic leadership," he is quoted as saying at the conference. "It directly correlates to the fact that people at Timberland are mission-centered, passionate people. What we do is makes boots and shoes. Who we are, is people who believe in the intersection of commerce and justice."

Each year Timberland conducts a survey to assess how they are doing in their employees' eyes. In the 2005 survey approximately 70% of them stated that the company's commitment to community plays a strong role in their decision to stay with the company.

149

Approximately 80% said they feel good about the ways in which Timberland contributes to the community. So what does the company do that is so special? Timberland strategically partners with City Year, a non-profit volunteering organization, and promotes employee involvement in the community.

Founded in 1988 City Year engages youth aged 17 to 24 in 10 months of community service and leadership development through their Youth Service Corps. The corps gets them involved in tutoring and mentoring school children, reclaiming public spaces, organizing after-school programs and developing curricula on important social issues. City Year and Timberland first met in 1989 when the former requested a donation of 50 pairs of work boots for its growing corps. Since then Timberland has invested millions of dollars in City Year. But the connection is not just about donating money and product; it is also about each enterprise offering value to the other.

Most significant to Timberland has been City Year's support in developing a culture of volunteerism among its employees. Timberland's widely praised and highly effective Path of Service™ program was developed by Swartz and inspired by City Year. Path of Service™ encourages volunteering by offering each employee 40 hours of paid volunteer time each year or even a paid long-term service sabbatical. In 2005 some 68% of Timberland's 5,600 employees took advantage of the program. Since its inception in 1992 Timberland employees have invested more than 330,000 volunteer hours with non-profit organizations in over 27 countries.

Providing the paid volunteer hours is one thing, but employees still have to decide when and where to get involved. For some it is easy. They already have a cause they are passionate about. Others look to the company for guidance. With the help of City Year, Timberland runs a number of programs in which employees may participate. The Community Builders Tour stops in different cities each year, partnering with local non-profit organizations and community members to paint murals, plant gardens or do whatever else the communities deem to be a priority. Serv-a-Palooza is a global annual event at which volunteers may clean and repair schools and community centers, revitalize parks and green spaces and participate in other projects to create a positive impact on communities and the environment.

Timberland's strategic partnering with City Year and its diligent, multi-faceted approach to community service generate many measurable benefits for the company. But ultimately the partnership is about people. The Timberland approach to good corporate citizenship provides "employees the opportunity to experience the power of working together for positive change."

TIM HORTONS: Personal Ownership Makes All the Difference

Tim Horton Children's Foundation

Tim Hortons store owners and employees really know the meaning of "rolling up their sleeves" to make a difference — they've been doing it for 32 years. There is no requirement to get involved and to participate in Tim Horton Children's Foundation activities, yet one hundred percent of Tim Hortons stores are making sure that kids in need have the opportunity to reach their potential by going to camp.

Unlike many companies with a top down approach to corporate philanthropy, Tim Hortons stores have always led the charge in making the foundation a hugely successful non-profit, which today sends over 11,000 kids to camp. Beginning with just 40 stores and a single camp, the foundation has grown to six camps — with contributions outstripping sales growth.

When the iconic hockey player and Tim Hortons co-founder died in a car crash in 1974 the company's co-founder, Ron Joyce, wanted a way to recognize the contributions and memory of his friend and partner. Joyce created the Tim Horton Children's Foundation with a focus on providing camping experiences for children in financial need. The decision to help deserving children foster confidence in their abilities was a natural way for Joyce to honor Tim Horton.

After all Horton had himself come from very humble beginnings and had always supported children's causes.

From the beginning store owners have been responsible for working with local agencies to identify local kids who could benefit most from a camp experience. Stores that identify local children are considered the kids' sponsors or their local home base. Each store takes particular pride in sending local kids off to thrive in an unparalleled camp experience.

Corporate executives and employees provide support through participation on the board, marketing, soliciting in-kind donations and volunteer support on Camp Day and Work Weekends. They participate in key events throughout the year, such as the camp's closing banquet. But store owners are the real driving force.

Owners and employees lead the charge in providing direct support for camps, through donations and volunteer efforts. The single biggest fundraising day for the foundation is the annual Camp Day fundraiser, when all coffee profits go directly to fund kids camp experiences. Camp Day has become the single most popular day to work in Tim Hortons stores. Employees clamor for a spot on the schedule, and Tim Horton executives give their day to working side-by-side with them.

Some may think that contributing coffee funds is a substantial enough contribution, but store owners and employees don't stop there. On their own initiative they use Camp Day to set up barbecues in the parking lot, run karaoke contests and operate car washes to raise even more funds in support of the foundation's work. Last year store owners and employees were responsible for raising $7.2 million in donations.

Beyond their generous financial support store owners and employees play a special role in getting the camp set up for kids. On Work Weekend they volunteer to make log-beds, clean boats and plant flowers. They work with family members, community members and partners to support the foundation's efforts. And the effort pays off. Campers arrive at their home-away-from-home, and local stores get to feel part of making kids camps just a little more special. In fact a recent Work Weekend drew over 1,200 participants.

Camp attendees and alumni, who have had the experience of attending one of the foundation's six camps, are invited to several events where store owners and employees are given insight into the difference their hard work makes in the lives of children. Alumni who are invited to speak at regional meetings are always met with roaring standing ovations. As foundation executive director Dave Newnham recalls, when alumni thank Tim Hortons for making their summer special, corporate executives, employees and owners alike feel they are the ones who should thank the kids for making them "feel like they are really making an important difference."

And Newnham knows what this means to the whole Tim Hortons team, for whom the foundation is "a real source of pride." This pride, says Newnham, can't be manufactured. "People see right through the marketing approach to philanthropy. This was just done on heart and soul," and that, he says, has made all the difference.

Because the foundation was built on Ron Joyce's belief that it was the "right thing to do," it has won the support of the entire company. As Newnham states, the work of the foundation is "just part of our culture." It creates pride, ownership and a personal investment in the company vision.

VANCITY: Rooted and Reaching — One Hand in the Soil, One Hand Grasping for the Stars

Beyond a Credit Union and Beyond Philanthropy

When you visit the home page of Vancity's Website (vancity.com) it's easy to forget that the company is a financial institution. With links to climate change solutions, advice on making sustainable purchasing decisions for your business, an online community blog focused on change and an opportunity to vote for the winner of the annual $1-million Vancity Award, you can get lost in the opportunity to make a difference.

As a member-owned institution British Columbia's Vancity prides itself on being "beyond the bank" and "beyond the credit union." One key factor that distinguishes Vancity from others in the crowded financial-services marketplace is its ability to think holistically and take the long view. While banks worry about quarterly profits Vancity focuses on what's best for its business, its members and the communities it serves in the long term. This long-term view supports a strong focus on community leadership.

"Community service is just part of our DNA," said Dave Mowat, Vancity's CEO, in an Orenda interview. "We look for opportunities to use our business and financial resources and expertise, and to partner with others, to make a positive difference in our communities."

In fact donations to its members and the community represent 30% of Vancity's total net earnings. Mowat puts it this way: "We run a good business so we can do good things for our members and our community."

Good business, indeed. VanCity is Canada's largest credit union, with $12 billion in assets, more than 345,000 members and 2,300 employees. Mowat attributes VanCity's success to the full integration of business, social and environmental objectives.

Describing the company's six business drivers he uses three fingers on his right hand to illustrate what makes Vancity different — Member Experience, Employee Experience and Community Leadership — and three fingers on his left hand to show what drives business — Membership Growth, Deepening Relationships and Financial Sustainability. As he interlocks his fingers he comments that the six drivers linked together are what make Vancity work. A chain is only as strong as its weakest link, he says. If one of those drivers is missing or not attended to, the company suffers.

In determining how best to focus its philanthropic dollars Vancity decided it should focus on its strengths by providing financial grants and awards to create strong non-profits and social enterprises throughout British Columbia. From grants to create more after-school programming for kids in Port Coquitlam to supporting an organization working to increase the employability of people with developmental disabilities in Burnaby, Vancity's financial support is impacting lives on a local level.

The company's commitment to its stakeholders also extends to its employees. The company has been repeatedly lauded as one of Canada's best places to work, getting the top ranking in this category in *Canadian Business* magazine. While other companies offer access to company-owned resorts and vacation time, Vancity invests where it counts by supporting full-tuition reimbursement for employees and an employee advisory committee.

An important element of the company's approach to employee engagement is meaningfully involving employees in its support of community and environment initiatives. In fact 91% of Vancity

employees say what Vancity does for the community and environment makes them "feel good about working here."

Vancity employees not only are kept informed about the local
initiatives that receive a boost from its philanthropic contributions,
they also are given the opportunity to become directly involved in
all levels of the company's community-giving strategy. In fact the
credit union's Community Leadership strategy is run by a team of
employees who represent all levels of the company. In addition
Vancity demonstrates its commitment to employee engagement in
the community by supporting non-profit ventures that can provide
volunteer opportunities for their employees.

The ultimate demonstration of Vancity's belief in the integral
role of employees in driving philanthropic decisions, however,
is its annual staff fundraiser. For over 20 years employees have
been given the opportunity to select one charity each year to be the
recipient of donations collected through personal donations, book
and bake sales, auctions and events. To date Vancity has collected
over $1.5 million for charities, including the Terry Fox Foundation
and Sunny Hill Hospital. And as part of its commitment to giving
back Vancity uses its "I gave at the office" program to match all
employee donations.

Given the multiple and tangible ways that Vancity leverages its
philanthropy program it is clear that its employees "believe" that
it is clearly a company that cares — about them, its members and
about the communities where it operates.

ZINGERMAN'S: Doing the Right Thing

The Quiet Contribution at Zingerman's

Zingerman's Delicatessen started out as a small specialty shop in Ann Arbor, Michigan, and has grown to become the Zingerman's Community of Businesses (zcob) — eight different businesses, each with its own specialty and all of them within the Ann Arbor area.

Visit the Zingerman's Website and you will find no mention of the company's corporate giving. Dig deep and you may find, in its newsletter, a promotion for a local fundraising event — but that's about it. It will not mention Zingerman's involvement in the event or its support of the charity. Low-profile corporate giving is the policy at Zingerman's. It opposes "using public acts of social responsibility as a way to enhance [its] image or products." It believes that the right to operate a business is earned by "doing the right thing," and it accepts responsibility to be a good citizen, "a reliable neighbor who works to improve educational, cultural and civic vitality." So while the company's philanthropic effort benefits many stakeholders, it is not specifically developed or promoted for corporate gain.

"The leader's number-one responsibility is to serve the organization — not the other way around," says the co-founder of Zingerman's, Ari Weinzweig. A culture of serving has been created at Zingerman's using the management theories of Robert Greenleaf and his concept of servant leadership. This affects how management supervises staff, how customers are treated and how the company operates within the community.

Community is important because it is at the core of everything

Zingerman's does. The company opened in 1982. Ten years later, as Ari and co-founder Paul Saginaw were deciding how to grow their business, they made community central to their decision. Rather than expand the company beyond its home of Ann Arbor, Michigan, they decided to create new, related companies. Zingerman's Community of Businesses was born. ZCoB now includes eight companies that are all co-owned by their managing partners and the founders of Zingerman's. A common factor behind the success of each company is a commitment to the Ann Arbor community.

In 1988 Paul conceived and championed the formation of Food Gatherers. Being in the food industry he could see just how much was thrown away every day. Zingerman's set up Food Gatherers to rescue perishable food from restaurants and stores and distribute it to shelters, detoxification programs, the Salvation Army and neighborhood meal programs, all in Ann Arbor.

Since its inception Food Gatherers has grown by applying many of the management techniques employed at Zingerman's itself. In 2005 it gathered and distributed over two million pounds of food. It now serves over 180 community organizations in Washtenaw County. The charity is supported by donations and community events like Rockin' for the Hungry and Grillin' for Food Gatherers, as well as complementary programs such as Plant a Row and Community Kitchen. Plant a Row encourages local gardeners and farmers to donate fresh produce to Food Gatherers. Community Kitchen takes any fresh produce that cannot be used immediately and makes sauces and meals that can be stored for later use. It also doubles as a job-training center, offering youths a free six-week course in the culinary arts while taking the pressure off the Kitchen's volunteers.

When speaking about the importance of the Ann Arbor community to Zingerman's Ari uses the French term *terroir*, which denotes the special characteristics that geography bestows on a food product such as wine. Take Zingerman's out of Ann Arbor, out of the community it was designed to serve commercially, out of the community it has supported philanthropically and the nature of the company would change, Ari says.

All of these initiatives and commitments have helped create a strong corporate culture, motivated employees and loyal customers. One cannot underestimate the value of customers who appreciate the company for its products as well as its generosity. This sign, from 13 non-profits, was posted on the company's 20th anniversary:

> *From all of us to all of Zingerman's*
>
> *Thank you for feeding, sheltering,*
> *educating, uplifting, and*
> *inspiring an entire community.*
> *Happy birthday to a deli*
> *that makes a difference.*
>
> *From the many, many, many,*
> *people you help,*
> *With all our hearts.*

Ari is adamant that an organization needs to give back and can do so while being profitable. "The two are not mutually exclusive," he says. The proof of this statement is in the results, for as Zingerman's continues to grow as a commercial venture, its commitment to philanthropy also grows. Zingerman's is currently in the process of setting up a charitable foundation that will open even more opportunities to support their Ann Arbor community.

Conclusion

This book has been written to help business leaders harness the power of a corporate philanthropy program to transform their businesses, *with inspiration*, from the inside out. I hope it has accomplished that goal.

If workplaces become inspirational places people will feel connection and engagement and their lives will be a bit better. If they go on to do something to serve their communities then communities will be a bit better. If corporations, employees, non-profits and government link arms, the quality of everyone's life will be better and the world will be a better place.

When it comes to corporate karma, John, Paul, George and Ringo said it best:

... the love you take ... is equal to the love you make

Sources

1 / ON A CLEAR DAY I CAN SEE AFRICA: THE ORENDA STORY

Websites
Avon: www.avoncompany.com/women/avoncrusade
Children's Hunger Fund™: www.childrenshungerfund.org
An Inconvenient Truth: www.climatecrisis.net
LensCrafters: www.givethegiftofsight.org
Global Partners for Development: www.gpfd.org
Oprah's Angel Network: www.oprahsangelnetwork.org
Timberland: www.timberland.com/timberlandserve
USANA Health Sciences: www.usana.com
Virgin: www.virgin.com

Books
Gore, Al. *An Inconvenient Truth: The Planetary Emergency of
    Global Warming and What We Can Do About It.* Rodale, 2006.
Hawken, Paul. *The Ecology of Commerce: A Declaration of Sustain-
    ability.* Collins Business, 1993.

Klein, Eric and Izzo, John. *Awakening Corporate Soul: Four Paths to Unleash the Power of People at Work.* Fairwinds Press, 1998.

2 / FINDING YOUR EMOTIONAL PROFIT CENTER: THE NEW CORPORATE PHILANTHROPY

Websites
Avon: www.avon.com
Compassionate Eye Foundation: www.compassionateeye.org
Cone: The 2004 Cone Corporate Citizenship Study:
www.coneinc.com/Pages/pr_30.html
Deloitte and Touche:
http://www.csrwire.com/PressRelease.php?id=3106
LensCrafters: www.lenscrafters.com
Manifest Communications: www.manifestcom.com
Merck: www.merck.com
Pampered Chef: www.pamperedchef.com
Reputation Institute: www.reputationinstitute.com
Robert Kent Photography: www.robertkentphoto.com
Spectrum Health Care: www.spectrumhealthcare.com
Timberland: www.timberland.com
Universum: http://phatgnat.com/log/2005/June/16/167/
Zingerman's: www.zingermans.com

Articles
Friedman, Milton. "The Social Responsibility of Business Is to Increase Its Profits." *The New York Times Magazine*, September 13, 1970.
Kelly, Marjorie. "Holy Grail Found: Absolute, Positive, Definitive Proof CSR Pays Off Financially." *Business Ethics*, winter 2004.
McClimon, Timothy J. "The Current State of Corporate Philanthropy." Donors Forum of Wisconsin conference transcript, April 8, 2005.
www.nyrag.org/usr_doc/Donors_Forum_of_Wisconsin_2005.doc

Porter, Michael E. and Kramer, Mark. "The Competitive Advantage of Corporate Philanthropy." *Harvard Business Review*, December 2002.

Wall Street Journal. "The Perils of Corporate Philanthropy." *Wall Street Journal*, January 16, 2002.

Books

Austin, James. E. *The Collaboration Challenge: How Nonprofits and Businesses Succeed Through Strategic Alliances*. Jossey-Bass, 2000.

Christopher, Doris. *The Pampered Chef: The Story of One of America's Most Beloved Companies*. Doubleday Currency, 2005.

Collins, Jim and Porras, Jerry. *Built to Last: Successful Habits of Visionary Companies*. HarperCollins, 1994.

Handy, Charles. *The Hungry Spirit: Beyond Capitalism*. Bantam Dell, 1999.

Izzo, John B. and Withers, Pam: *Values Shift: The New Work Ethic and What It Means for Business*. Fairwinds Press, 2001.

Secretan, Lance. *Inspire! What Great Leaders Do*. John Wiley, 2004.

3 / STEP #1: LEAD WITH INSPIRATION

Websites

Secretan Center: www.secretan.com

Spectrum Health Care: www.spectrumhealthcare.com

Timberland: www.timberland.com

USANA Health Sciences: www.usana.com

Articles

Lowe, Graham. "Trust Is Tops: How You Can Build a Better Workplace Culture." *Canadian Business*, April 10-23, 2006.

Books

Secretan, Lance. *Inspire! What Great Leaders Do*. John Wiley, 2004.

4 / Step #2: Connect Company and Cause

Websites

Avon Foundation: www.avonfoundation.org

Boundless Playgrounds: www.boundlessplaygrounds.org

Children's Hunger Fund™: www.childrenshungerfund.org

Choice Humanitarian: www.choicehumanitarian.org

City Year: www.cityyear.org

Doe Fund: www.doe.org

Ericsson Response: www.ericsson.com/ericsson/corporate_responsibility/
ericssonresponse

Evergreen: www.evergreen.ca

Gift of Sight: www.givethegiftofsight.org

Habitat for Humanity: www.habitat.org

Hasbro: www.hasbro.com

M·A·C Cosmetics Aids Fund: www.macaidsfund.org

Millennium Promise: www.millenniumpromise.org

Spectrum Health Care: www.spectrumhealthcare.com

Timberland: www.timberland.com

United Nations Millennium Project: www.unmillenniumproject.org

USANA Health Sciences: www.usana.com

Zingerman's: www.zingermans.com

Foundation Resources

San Diego Grantmakers: www.sdgrantmakers.org

Association for Small Foundations: www.smallfoundations.org

Foundation Group: www.501c3.org

Hurwit and Associates: www.hurwitassociates.com

Philanthropic Foundations Canada: www.pfc.ca

San Diego Grantmakers: www.sdgrantmakers.org

Books

Twist, Lynne. *The Soul of Money: Transforming Your Relationship
with Money and Life.* Norton, 2003.

5 / Step #3: Get Everyone Involved

Websites
City Year: www.cityyear.org
Compassionate Eye Foundation: www.compassionateeye.org
Gift of Sight: www.givethegiftofsight.org
Global Partners for Development: www.gpfd.org
The Home Depot: www.homedepot.com
Isagenix International: www.isagenix.com
KaBoom!: www.kaboom.org
Luxottica: www.luxoticca.com
M·A·C Cosmetics: www.maccosmetics.com
M·A·C Aids Fund: www.macaidsfund.org
Millennium Promise: www.millenniumpromise.org
Pampered Chef: www.pamperedchef.com
Robert Kent Photography: www.robertkentphoto.com
Roots: www.roots.com
Spectrum Health Care: www.spectrumhealthcare.com
Timberland: www.timberland.com
USANA Health Sciences: www.usana.com
World Wildlife Fund: www.worldwildlifefund.org

6 / Step #4: Start Spreading the News

Websites
Children's Hunger Fund: www.childrenshungerfund.org
Choice Humanitarian: www.choicehumanitarian.org
Cone: The 2004 Cone Corporate Citizenship Study:
    www.coneinc.com/ Pages/pr_30.html
Gift of Sight: www.givethegiftofsight.org
Manifest Communications: www.manifestcom.com
Nine Million: www.ninemillion.org
Oprah's Angel Network: www.oprah.com/uyl/angel
Spectrum Health Care: www.spectrumhealthcare.com
USANA Health Sciences: www.usana.com

Articles
Williams, Natalia. "Good Business." *Strategy Magazine*, August 2006.

Books
Kotler, Philip and Lee, Nancy. *Corporate Social Responsibility*. Wiley, 2005.

7 / Step #5: Measure and Grow

Websites
Children's Hunger Fund™: www.childrenshungerfund.org
Guidestar: www.guidestar.org
Imagine Canada: www.imaginecanada.ca

Books
Benioff, Marc and Southwick, Karen. *Compassionate Capitalism: How Corporations Can Make Doing Good an Integral Part of Doing Well*. Career Press, 2004.

8 / Can't Buy Me Love: The Evolution of the Workforce

Websites
Canadian Fundraiser Newsletter: www.canadianfundraiser.com
Cone: 2006 Cone Millennial Cause Study: www.coneinc.com/Pages/research.html
Graduation Pledge: www.graduationpledge.org
Lifeweb: Living System Design: www.sahtouris.com
Millennium Promise: www.millenniumpromise.org
Ryan Hreljac: www.ryanswell.ca

Articles
The Economist. "The Battle for Brainpower." *The Economist,* October 7, 2006.
Grow, Brian, Hamm, Steve and Lee, Louise. "The Debate Over Doing Good." *Business Week*, August, 2005.

Maich, Steve. "Canada's Top 100 Employers." *Maclean's*, October 16, 2006.

Rubin, Harriet. "Dr. Brilliant vs. the Devil of Ambition." *Fast Company*, September 2000.

Books

Izzo, John B. and Withers, Pam. *Values Shift: The New Work Ethic and What It Means for Business*. Fairwinds Press, 2001.

Wood, John. *Leaving Microsoft to Change the World: An Entrepreneur's Odyssey to Educate the World's Children*. New York: Collins, 2006.

9 / FROM COLLECTING TO COLLABORATING: THE NON-PROFIT MESSAGE

Websites

Children's Hunger Fund™: www.childrenshungerfund.org

Choice Humanitarian: www.choicehumanitarian.org

Spectrum Health Care: www.spectrumhealthcare.com

USANA Health Services: www.usana.com

Books

Austin, James E. *The Collaboration Challenge: How Nonprofits and Businesses Succeed Through Strategic Alliances*. Jossey-Bass, 2000.

10 / WALKING THE TALK: THE PATHFINDERS

(Listed in order of company profiles.)

Ericsson: www.ericsson.com

Hasbro: www.hasbro.com

Boundless Playgrounds: www.boundlessplaygrounds.org

The Home Depot: www.homedepot.com

KaBOOM!: www.kaboom.org

www.businessweek.com/magazine/content/05_33/b3947114_mz017.htm

www.volunteerprojects123.org/story12c9.html

Luxottica: www.luxottica.com
Lenscrafters: www.lenscrafters.com
Gift of Sight: www.givethegiftofsight.org
M.A.C Cosmetics: www.maccosmetics.com
M.A.C Aids Fund: www.macaidsfund.org
Robert Kent Photography: www.robertkentphoto.com
Compassionate Eye Foundation:www.compassionateeye.org
Getty Images: www.gettyimages.com
Spectrum Health Care: www.spectrumhealthcare.com
Timberland: www.timberland.com
City Year: www.cityyear.org
    www.philanthropy.com/free/articles/v17/i14/14003501.htm
Tim Hortons: www.timhortons.com
Vancity: www.vancity.com
Zingerman's: www.zingermans.com

Recommended Reading

Adler, Stephen M. *Cause for Concern: Results-Oriented Cause Marketing*. Thomson/South-Western, 2006.

Arena, Christine. *Cause for Success: 10 Companies That Put Profit Second and Came in First*. New World Library, 2004.

Austin, James E. *The Collaboration Challenge: How Nonprofits and Businesses Succeed Through Strategic Alliances*. Jossey-Bass, 2000.

Benioff, Marc and Southwick, Karen. *Compassionate Capitalism: How Corporations Can Make Doing Good an Integral Part of Doing Well*. Career Press, 2004.

Burlingham, Bo. *Small Giants: Companies That Choose to Be Great Instead of Big*. Penguin Group, 2005.

Cohen, Ben and Warwick, Mal. *Values-Driven Business: How to Change the World, Make Money and Have Fun*. Berrett-Koehler, 2006.

Hawken, Paul. *The Ecology of Commerce: A Declaration of Sustainability*. Collins Business, 1993.

Hollender, Jeffrey and Fenichell, Stephen. *What Matters Most: How a Small Group of Pioneers Is Teaching Social Responsibility to Big Business, and Why Big Business Is Listening*. Basic Books, 2004.

Izzo, John B. and Withers, Pam: *Values Shift: The New Work Ethic and What It Means for Business*. Fairwinds Press, 2001.

Klein, Eric and Izzo, John. *Awakening Corporate Soul: Four Paths to Unleash the Power of People at Work*. Fairwinds Press, 1998.

Paine, Lynn Sharp. *Value Shift: Why Companies Must Merge Social and Financial Responsibility to Achieve Superior Performance*. McGraw-Hill, 2003.

Sachs, Jeffrey D. *The End of Poverty: Economic Possibilities for Our Time*. Penguin Books, 2005.

Secretan, Lance. *Inspire! What Great Leaders Do*. John Wiley, 2004.

Secretan, Lance: *One: The Art and Practice of Conscious Leadership*. The Secretan Center, 2006.

Twist, Lynne. *The Soul of Money: Transforming Your Relationship with Money and Life*. W.W. Norton, 2003.

Wood, John. *Leaving Microsoft to Change the World: An Entrepreneur's Odyssey to Educate the World's Children*. Collins, 2006.

ABOUT ORENDA

Consulting Services

Orenda is a strategic corporate philanthropy consulting company that helps companies leverage the power of corporate philanthropy to create a meaningful connection between people and the places they work. Orenda inspires companies to extend their vision beyond the balance sheet, providing them with the tools to move forward by giving back. Orenda customizes its approach to meet each client's unique situation. Services include:

- Company Assessment
- Program Development
- Event Planning
- Charity Evaluation
- Communication Strategy
- Program Integration

Speaking Topics That Will Inspire Your Audience

Moving Forward by Giving Back

Corporate philanthropy can unleash the potential of organizations by energizing employees, improving loyalty and retention, enhancing personal satisfaction and establishing trust. In this presentation Peggie Pelosi establishes the case for corporate philanthropy and lays out what it takes to create action plans that deliver meaningful results.

Connecting Company and Cause

Creating the right fit between a company and a charity will define the success of any corporate philanthropy initiative. The right fit requires an in-depth understanding of the needs of your company: what you offer, your core mission and your strengths and resources. It also requires asking key questions of a charitable organization that will ultimately define the longevity of the relationship.

Finding Your Company's *Emotional* Profit Center

Do your employees know about your corporate philanthropy partners? Are these messages coming from the right source? Are there opportunities for employees to roll up their sleeves and pitch in? Would your employees be willing to make a contribution — either by participating in an event, offering their skills or making a donation to the company's cause?

Can't Buy Me Love: The Evolution of the Workforce

The right corporate philanthropy strategy responds to the needs of young people by helping them see the "higher purpose" of their work beyond a paycheck. The latest research indicates that the new crop of talent expects corporations to play a role that was formerly the domain of governments, schools and civic organizations. In this presentation Peggie Pelosi provides a step-by-step plan for how to create corporate philanthropy programs that win the attention, commitment and loyalty of today's employees.

From Collecting to Collaborating: The Non-Profit Message

This presentation, designed for non-profit leaders, describes how great corporate-cause partnerships are about much more than giving and receiving money. They are about meshing missions, resources and skills to create a win-win-win — for the company, the non-profit and the world.

To contact Orenda:
e-mail: info@orendaconnections.com
phone: (416) 993-9383